# The Calvin and Hobbes
# LAZY SUNDAY BOOK

## A Collection of Sunday Calvin and Hobbes Cartoons
## by BILL WATTERSON

WARNER BOOKS

# To Rich West

A *Warner* Book

First published in Great Britain by Sphere Books Ltd 1990
Reprinted 1990, 1992
This edition published by Warner Books in 1992
Reprinted 1993, 1994 (twice), 1995, 1997, 1999, 2001

ISBN 0 7515 0894 2

Printed and bound in Great Britain by
The Bath Press, Bath

Warner Books
A Division of
Little, Brown and Company (UK)
Brettenham House
Lancaster Place
London WC2E 7EN

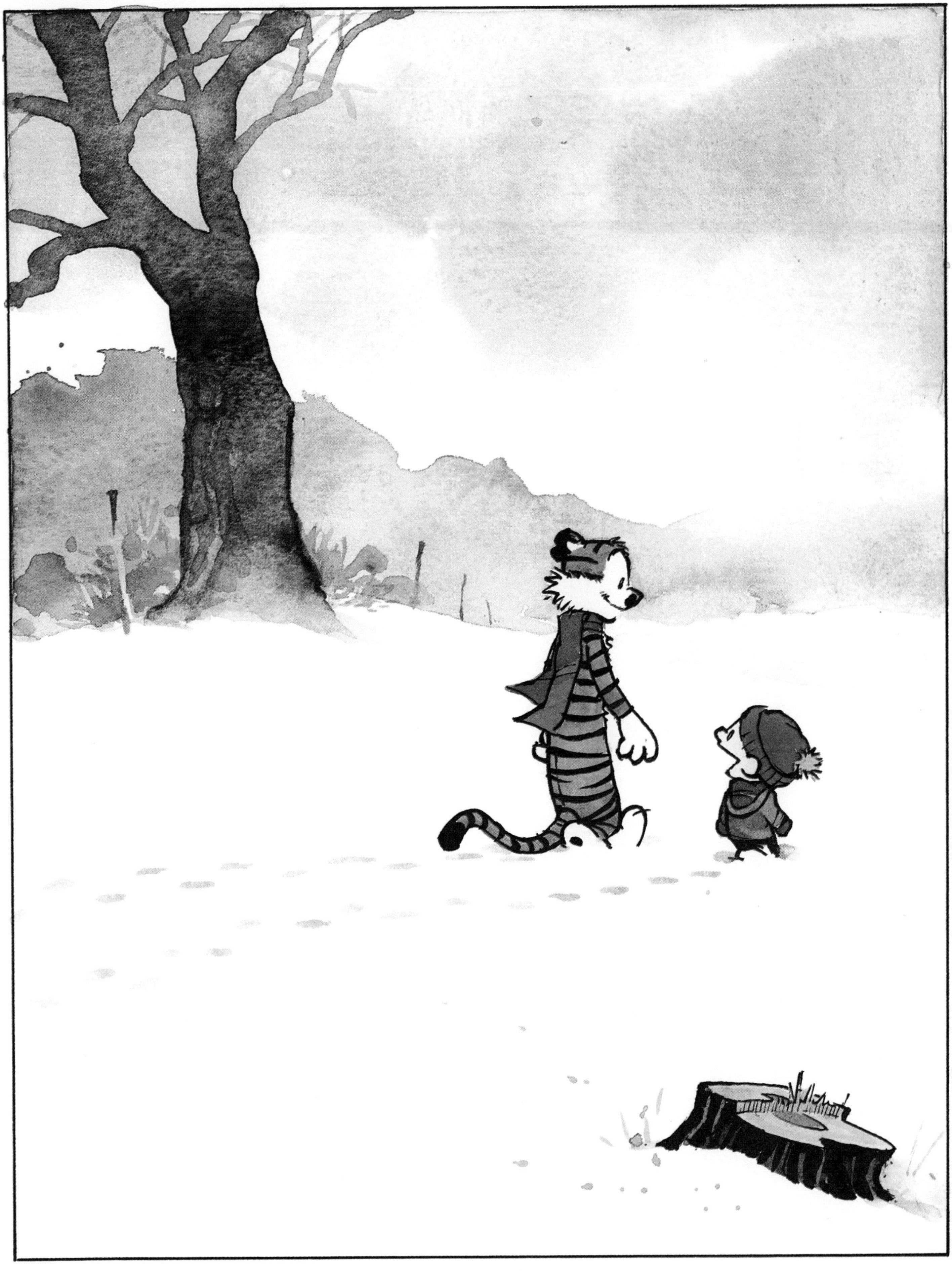

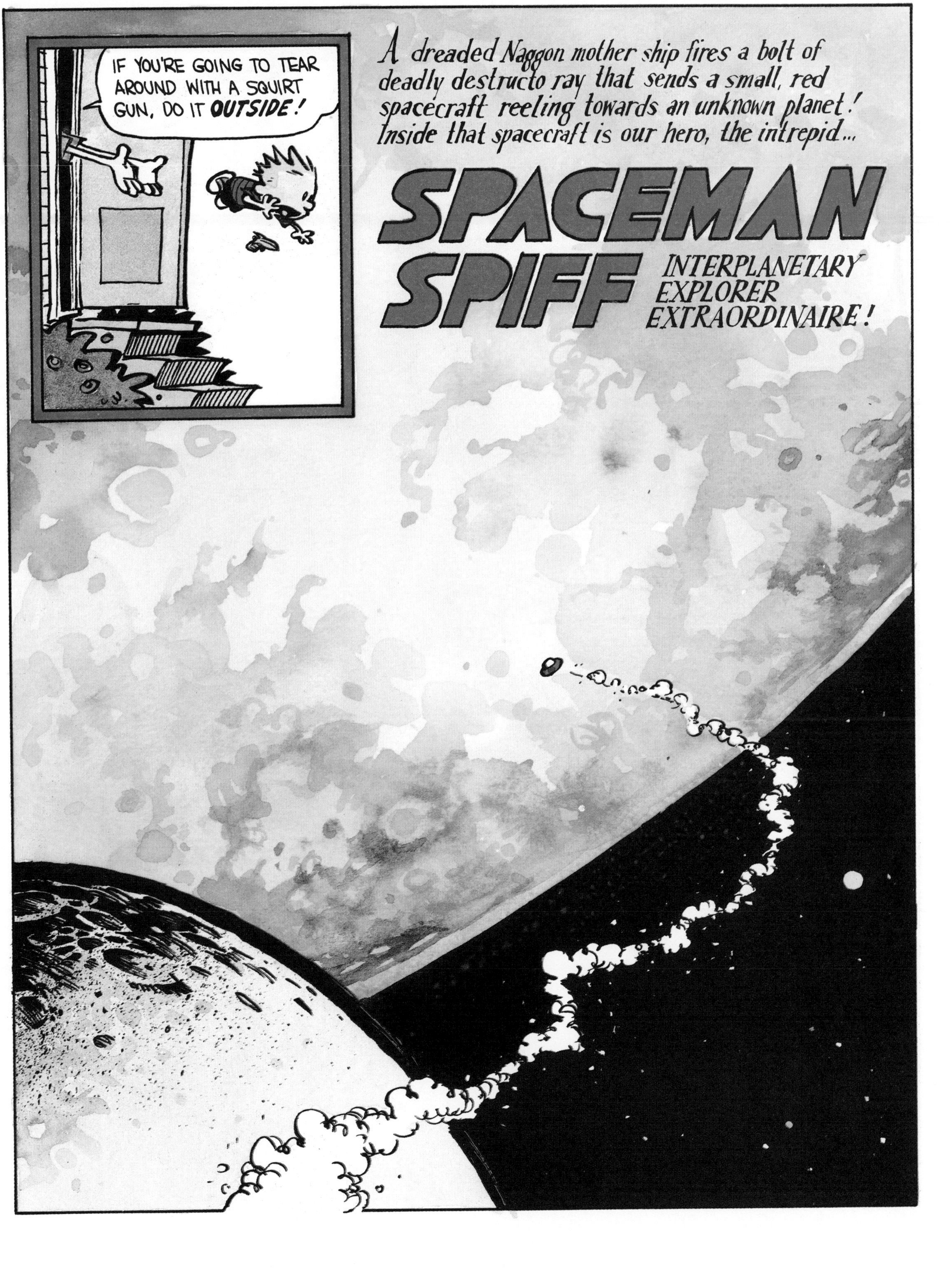
IF YOU'RE GOING TO TEAR AROUND WITH A SQUIRT GUN, DO IT OUTSIDE!
A dreaded Naggon mother ship fires a bolt of deadly destructo ray that sends a small, red spacecraft reeling towards an unknown planet! Inside that spacecraft is our hero, the intrepid...
SPACEMAN SPIFF
INTERPLANETARY EXPLORER EXTRAORDINAIRE!

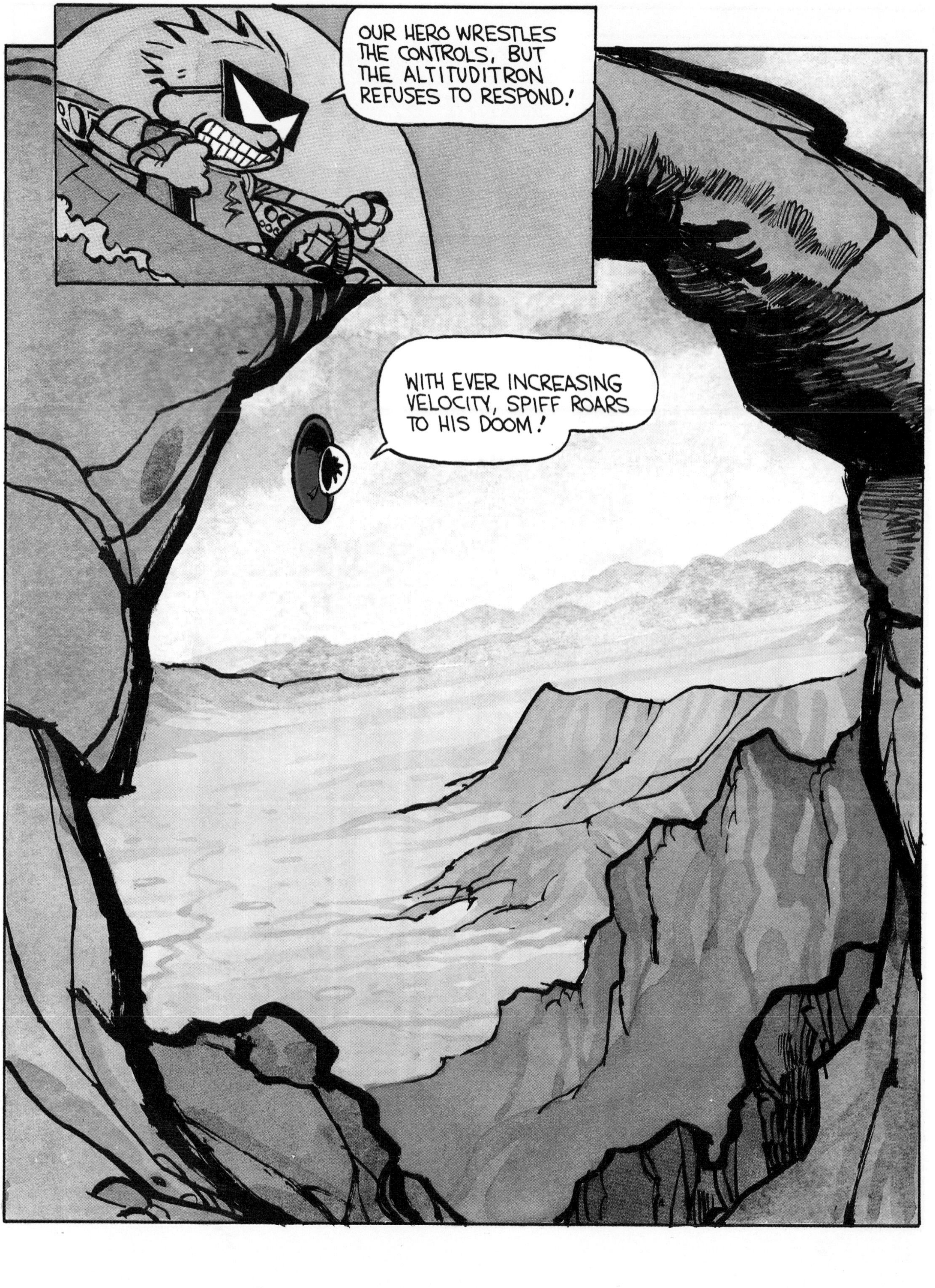
OUR HERO WRESTLES THE CONTROLS, BUT THE ALTITUDITRON REFUSES TO RESPOND!
WITH EVER INCREASING VELOCITY, SPIFF ROARS TO HIS DOOM!

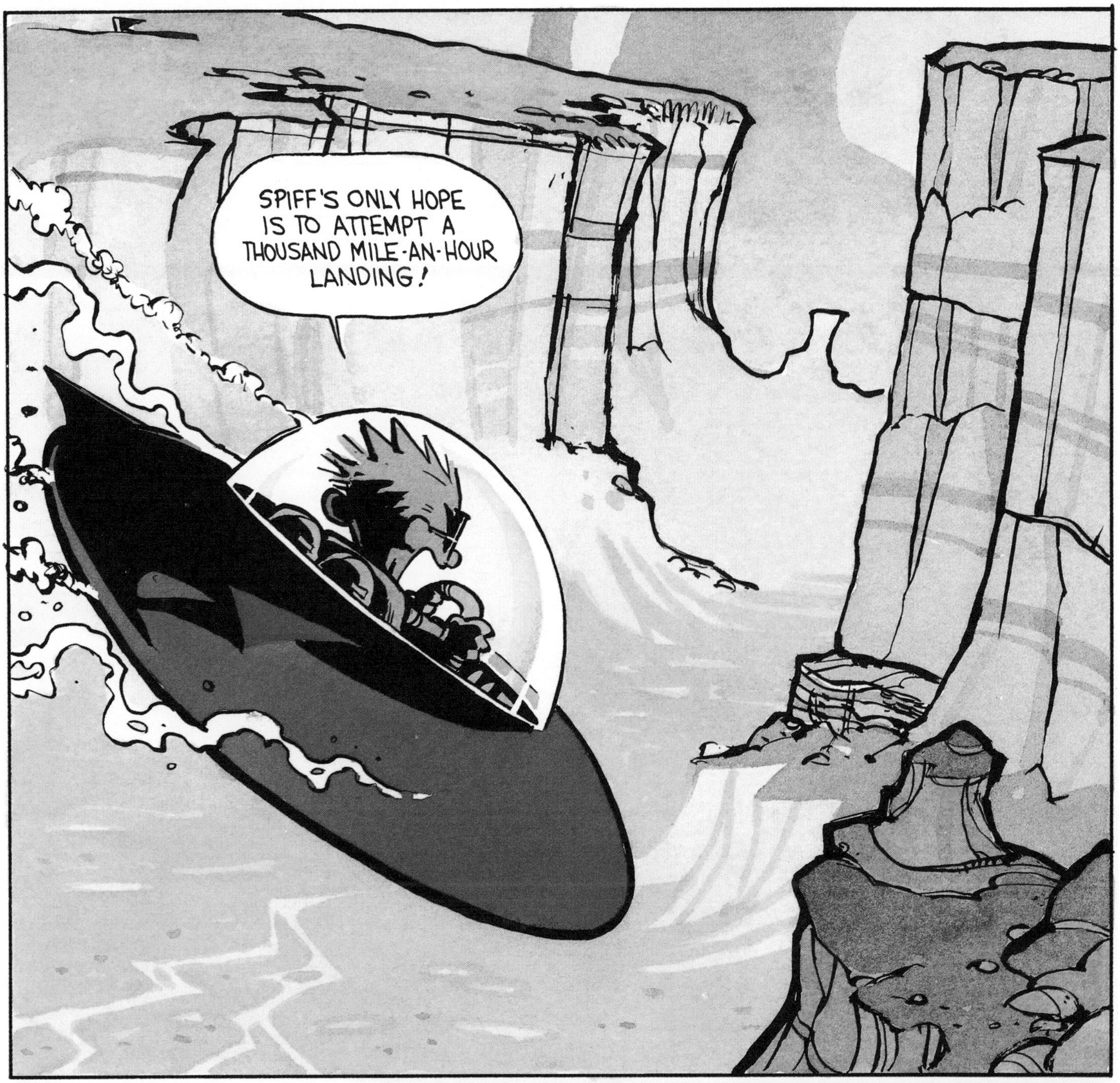
SPIFF'S ONLY HOPE IS TO ATTEMPT A THOUSAND MILE-AN-HOUR LANDING!

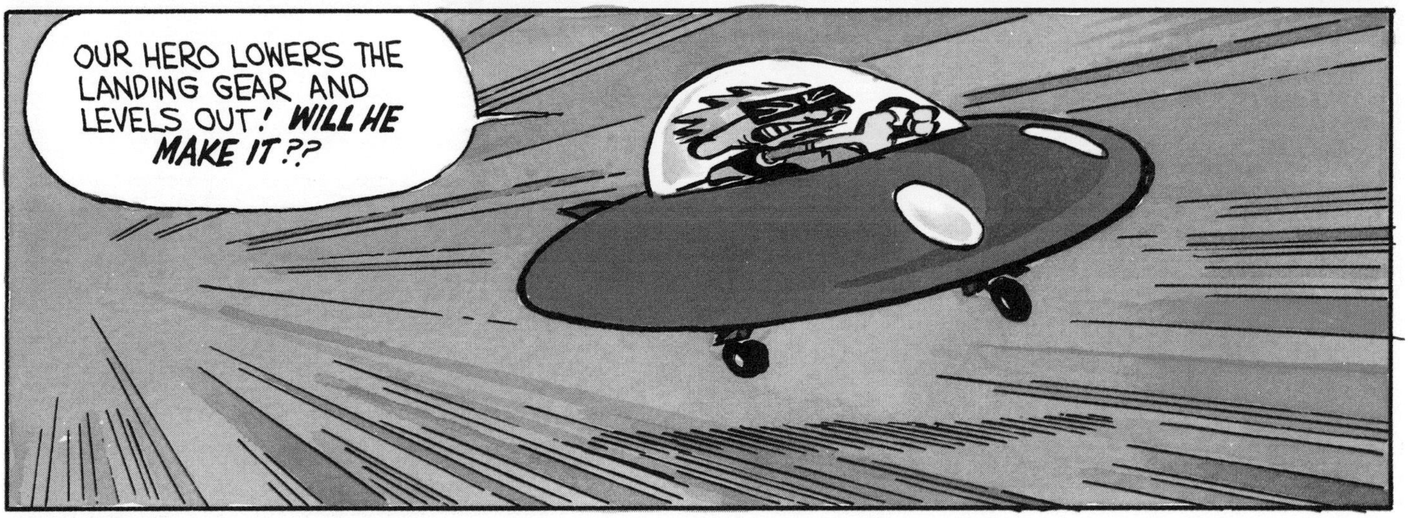
OUR HERO LOWERS THE LANDING GEAR AND LEVELS OUT! WILL HE MAKE IT??

HMPH.

YES! THE INCREDIBLE SPACEMAN SPIFF SURVIVES! DAZED, BUT UNHURT, OUR HERO CRAWLS FROM THE SMOLDERING WRECKAGE!

SPIFF SETS OFF ACROSS THE PLANET SURFACE. AN OMINOUS, SHADOWY FIGURE FLITS ACROSS A NEARBY HILLTOP! AN ALIEN!

OUR HERO DARTS BEHIND A ROCK AND SETS HIS ZORCHER ON "SHAKE AND BAKE." THE ALIEN APPROACHES!

HI CALVIN! I SEE YOU, SO YOU CAN STOP HIDING NOW! ARE YOU PLAYING COWBOYS OR SOMETHING? CAN I PLAY TOO?

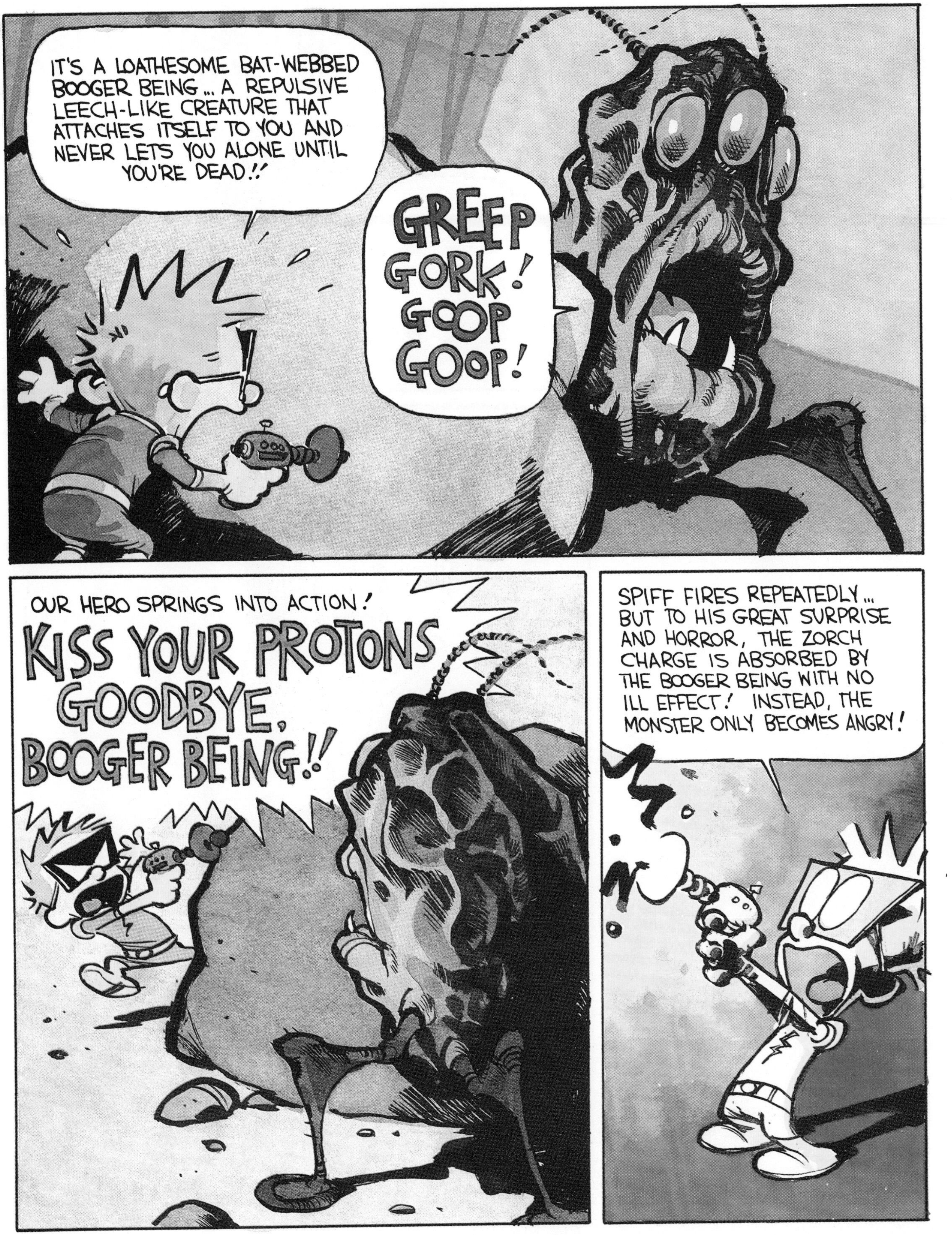
IT'S A LOATHESOME BAT-WEBBED BOOGER BEING... A REPULSIVE LEECH-LIKE CREATURE THAT ATTACHES ITSELF TO YOU AND NEVER LETS YOU ALONE UNTIL YOU'RE DEAD!!
GREEP GORK! GOOP GOOP!
OUR HERO SPRINGS INTO ACTION!
KISS YOUR PROTONS GOODBYE, BOOGER BEING!!
SPIFF FIRES REPEATEDLY... BUT TO HIS GREAT SURPRISE AND HORROR, THE ZORCH CHARGE IS ABSORBED BY THE BOOGER BEING WITH NO ILL EFFECT! INSTEAD, THE MONSTER ONLY BECOMES ANGRY!

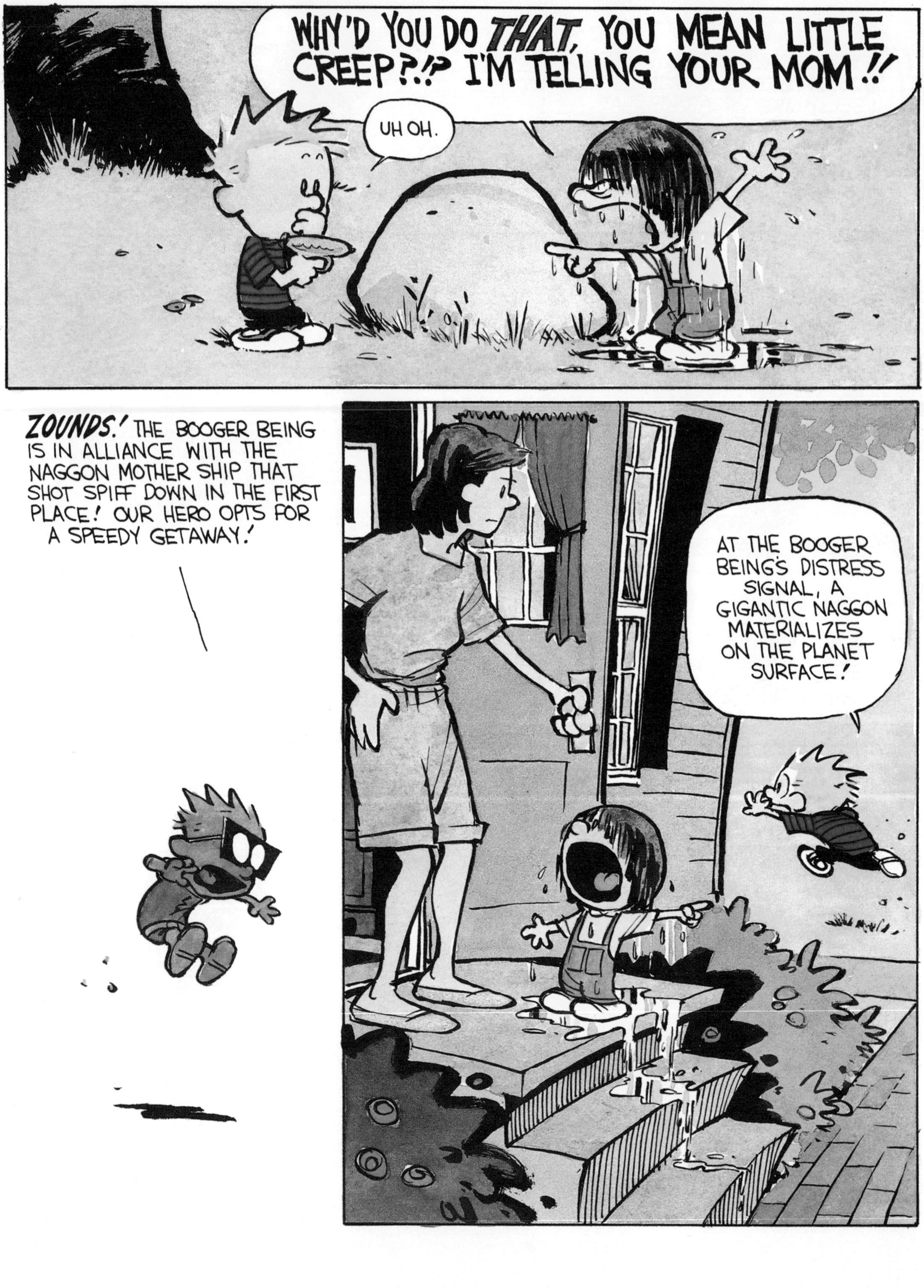
WHY'D YOU DO THAT, YOU MEAN LITTLE CREEP?!? I'M TELLING YOUR MOM!!
UH OH.
ZOUNDS! THE BOOGER BEING IS IN ALLIANCE WITH THE NAGGON MOTHER SHIP THAT SHOT SPIFF DOWN IN THE FIRST PLACE! OUR HERO OPTS FOR A SPEEDY GETAWAY!
AT THE BOOGER BEING'S DISTRESS SIGNAL, A GIGANTIC NAGGON MATERIALIZES ON THE PLANET SURFACE!

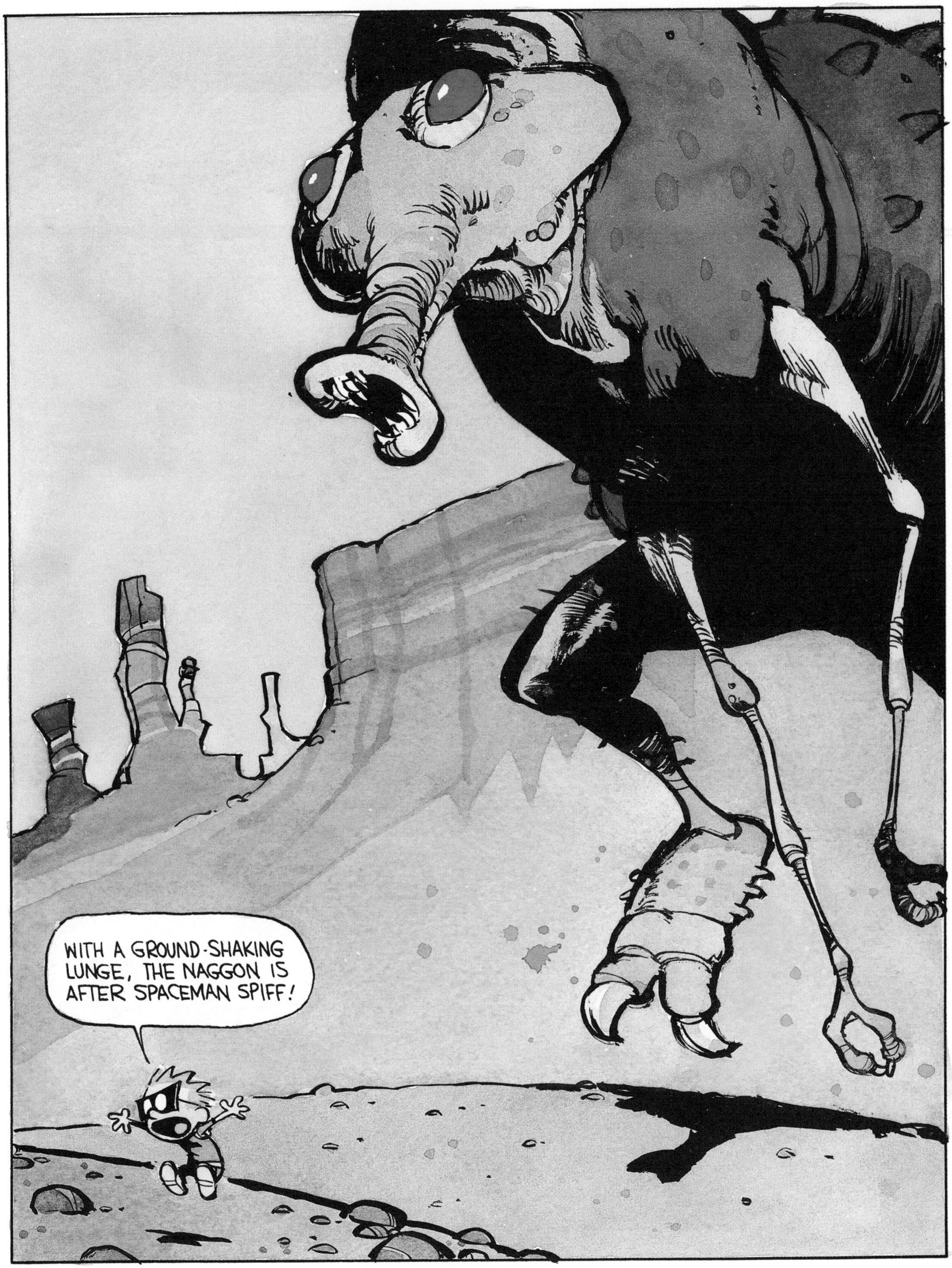
WITH A GROUND-SHAKING LUNGE, THE NAGGON IS AFTER SPACEMAN SPIFF!

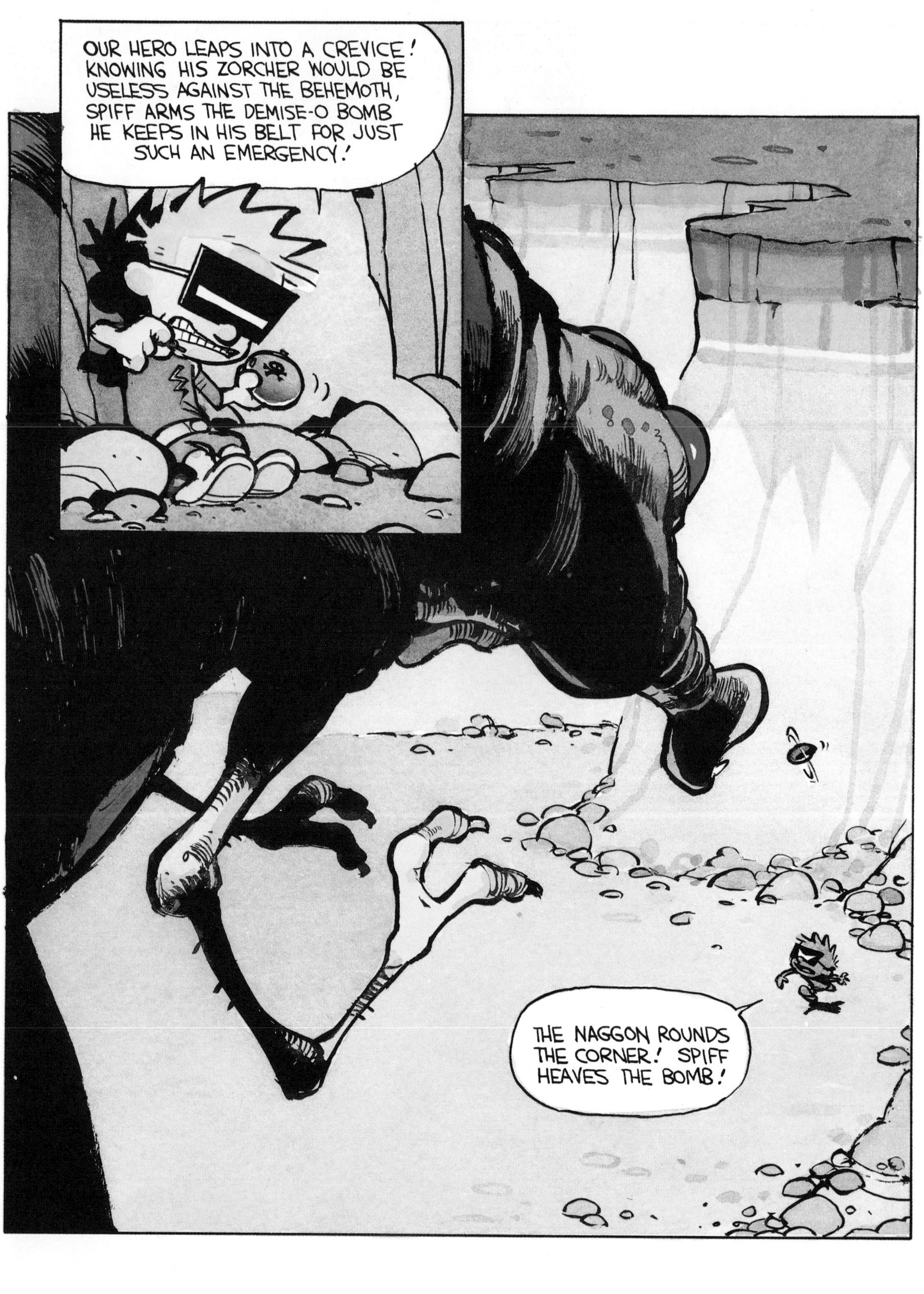
OUR HERO LEAPS INTO A CREVICE! KNOWING HIS ZORCHER WOULD BE USELESS AGAINST THE BEHEMOTH, SPIFF ARMS THE DEMISE-O BOMB HE KEEPS IN HIS BELT FOR JUST SUCH AN EMERGENCY!
THE NAGGON ROUNDS THE CORNER! SPIFF HEAVES THE BOMB!

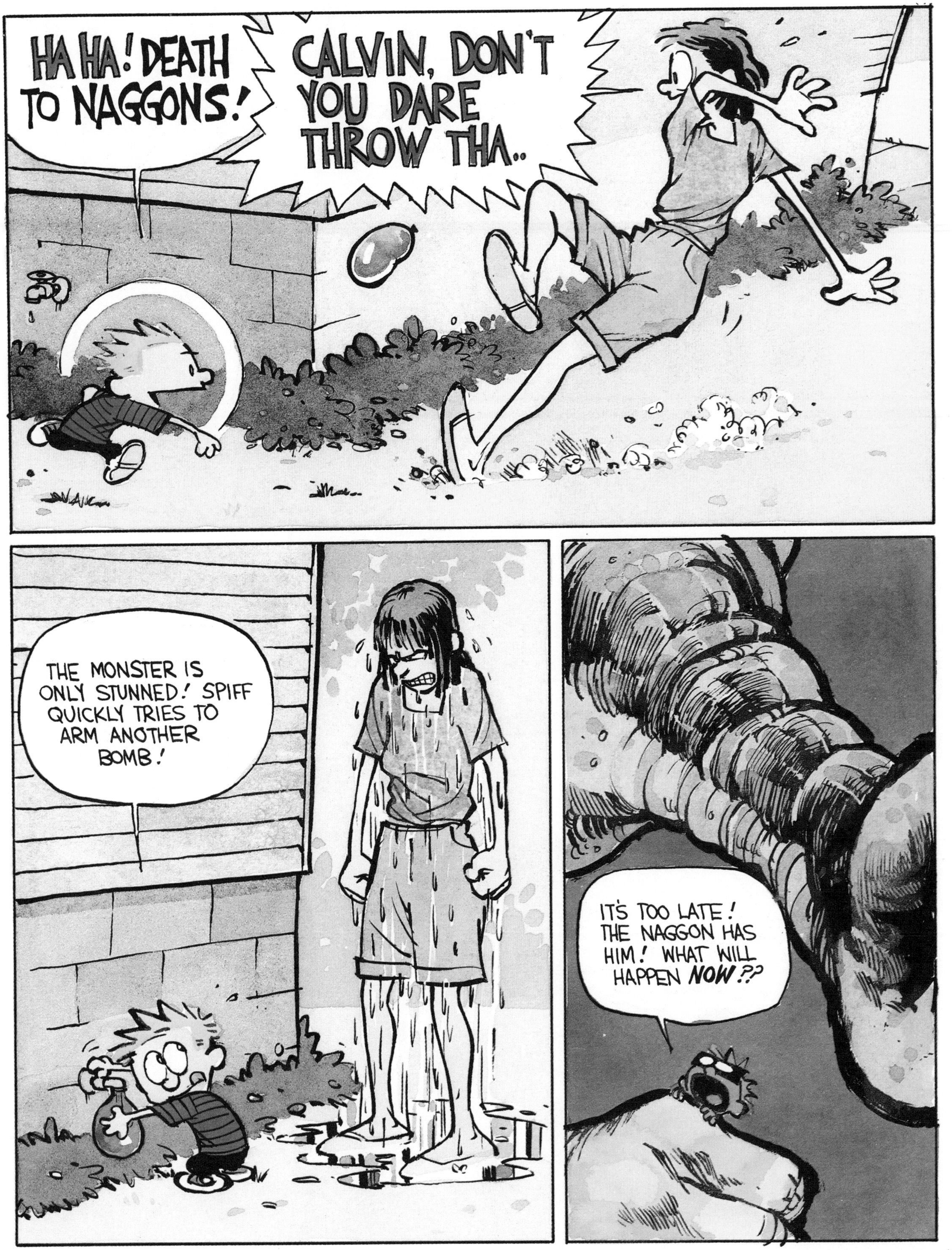
HA HA! DEATH TO NAGGONS!
CALVIN, DON'T YOU DARE THROW THA..
THE MONSTER IS ONLY STUNNED! SPIFF QUICKLY TRIES TO ARM ANOTHER BOMB!
IT'S TOO LATE! THE NAGGON HAS HIM! WHAT WILL HAPPEN NOW??

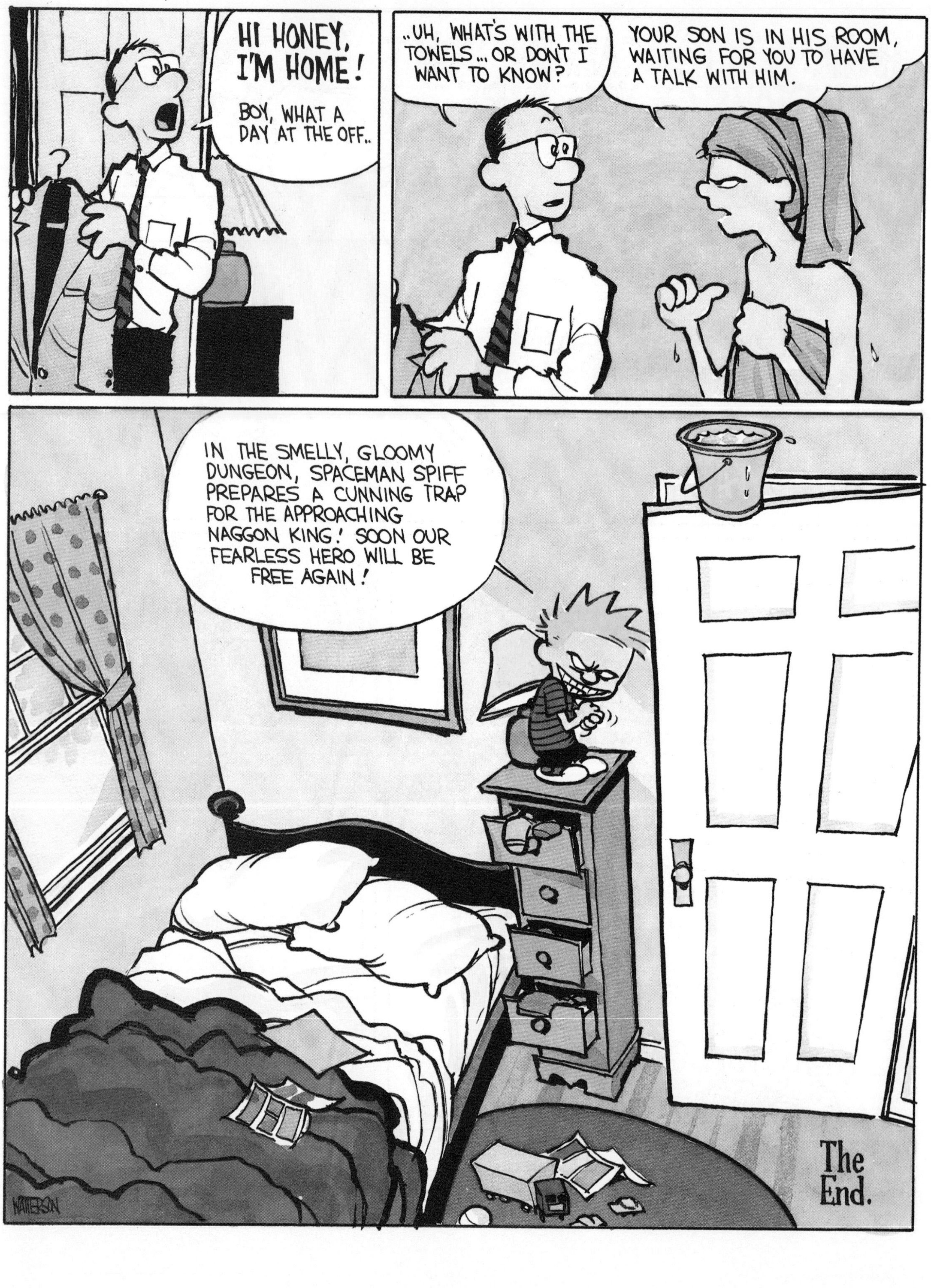
HI HONEY, I'M HOME!
BOY, WHAT A DAY AT THE OFF..
..UH, WHAT'S WITH THE TOWELS... OR DON'T I WANT TO KNOW?
YOUR SON IS IN HIS ROOM, WAITING FOR YOU TO HAVE A TALK WITH HIM.
IN THE SMELLY, GLOOMY DUNGEON, SPACEMAN SPIFF PREPARES A CUNNING TRAP FOR THE APPROACHING NAGGON KING! SOON OUR FEARLESS HERO WILL BE FREE AGAIN!
The End.
WATTERSON

# Calvin and Hobbes by WATERSON

"BEFORE BEGINNING ANY HOME-PLUMBING REPAIR, MAKE SURE YOU POSSESS THE PROPER TOOLS FOR THE JOB."

"CHECK THE FOLLOWING LIST OF HANDY EXPLETIVES, AND SEE THAT YOU KNOW HOW TO USE THEM."

CALVIN WAKES UP ONE MORNING TO FIND HE NO LONGER EXISTS IN THE THIRD DIMENSION! HE IS **2-D**!

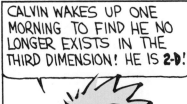

THINNER THAN A SHEET OF PAPER, CALVIN HAS NO SURFACE AREA ON THE BOTTOM OF HIS FEET! HE IS IMMOBILE!

ONLY BY "WAVING" HIS BODY CAN CALVIN CREATE ENOUGH FRICTION WITH THE GROUND TO MOVE!

HAVING WIDTH BUT NO THICKNESS, CALVIN IS VULNERABLE TO THE SLIGHTEST GUST OF WIND!

TO AVOID DRAFTS, HE TWISTS HIMSELF INTO A TUBE, AND ROLLS ACROSS THE FLOOR!

WATERSON

SOMEONE IS COMING! CALVIN QUICKLY STANDS UP STRAIGHT.

TURNING PERFECTLY SIDEWAYS, HE IS A NEARLY INVISIBLE VERTICAL LINE! NO ONE WILL NOTICE!

HEY DAD, KNOW WHY YOU DIDN'T SEE ME ALL MORNING?? I WAS TWO-DIMENSIONAL!

HMMM, I'LL BET YOU CAN'T DO IT ALL AFTERNOON, TOO...

DEAR!

# Calvin and Hobbes

by WATTERSON

# Calvin and Hobbes by WATTERSON

OY OH BOY OH BOY OH BOY OH BOY OH BOY OH BOY OH BOY OH BOY OH BOY OH BOY OH BOY

WAIT! WAIT! I'VE GOT TO SAVOR THIS MOMENT! THE BRILLIANCE OF IT ALL! I'M A GENIUS! A SHEER *GENIUS!*

SUSIE'S PLAYING ON THE SIDEWALK! NOW'S MY CHANCE TO USE THE SNOWBALL I'VE BEEN SAVING IN THE FREEZER!

SHE'LL NEVER EXPECT A SNOWBALL IN *JUNE!* BOY, WILL SHE BE MAD! HA HA HA!

THIS IS GOING TO BE GREAT! HERE IT COMES! OH BOY! OH BOY!

HEY SUSIE!!

PIFF

WATTERSON

I *MISSED!* DARN IT DARN IT DARN IT!! OF ALL THE MISERABLE LUCK!

AAARRGHH!

THERE MUST'VE BEEN A CROSS BREEZE! I CAN'T BELIEVE IT! I SAVED THAT SNOWBALL FOR THREE WHOLE MONTHS! I...

SCOOP SCOOP

I.. I...UH...

POW

THE IRONY OF THIS IS JUST SICKENING.

THE DREADED SCUM BEINGS FIRE! SPACEMAN SPIFF IS **HIT!**

IT NEVER FAILS. I JUST WASHED AND WAXED THIS THING.

OUR HERO, THE INTREPID SPACEMAN SPIFF, STRUGGLES WITH THE CONTROLS OF HIS DAMAGED SPACECRAFT!

THE FREEM PROPULSION BLASTERS ARE USELESS! SPIFF CRASHES ONTO THE SURFACE OF AN ALIEN PLANET!

UNSCATHED, THE FEARLESS SPACE EXPLORER EMERGES FROM THE SMOLDERING WRECKAGE! HE IS MAROONED ON A HOSTILE WORLD!

SCORCHED BY TWIN SUNS, THE PLANET IS NOTHING BUT BARREN ROCK AND METHANE! THERE'S NO HOPE OF FINDING FOOD OR WATER!

SPIFF COLLAPSES! OH NO, A HIDEOUS ALIEN SPOTS HIM! IN HIS WEAKENED STATE, SPIFF IS NO MATCH FOR THE MONSTER! **THIS COULD BE THE END!!**

LUNCHTIME! I BROUGHT YOU A SANDWICH AND SOME LEMONADE.

BRING THE DISHES BACK WHEN YOU'RE DONE, OK?

...OH WELL.

THANKS, MOM.

22

# Calvin and Hobbes
by WATTERSON

THE FIRE'S NOT LIGHTING, HUH?
CAN I MAKE A SUGGESTION?

GIVE UP ON THAT SISSY LIGHTER FLUID.

CAN'T WE COOK THE HAMBURGERS YET?

THE COALS AREN'T HOT ENOUGH.

BUT I'M HUNGRY! I WANT TO EAT *NOW!*

WELL, YOU'LL JUST HAVE TO WAIT.

YOU KNOW, CALVIN, SOMETIMES THE ANTICIPATION OF SOMETHING IS MORE FUN THAN THE THING ITSELF ONCE YOU GET IT.

HERE WE ARE, IT'S A BEAUTIFUL EVENING. IT'S NICE TO JUST SIT HERE AND LOOK AT THE TREES WHILE WE WAIT FOR THE COALS TO GET HOT, DON'T YOU THINK?

DINNER WILL BE OVER SOON, AND AFTERWARD WE'LL BE DISTRACTED WITH OTHER THINGS TO DO. BUT NOW WE HAVE A FEW MINUTES TO OURSELVES TO ENJOY THE EVENING.

THESE SUMMER DAYS GO BY SO QUICKLY. IT'S GOOD THAT EVERY NOW AND THEN WE HAVE TO WAIT FOR SOMETHING.

SO SHOULD I GO TO McDONALD'S THEN, OR WHAT?

YEAH, I KNOW. YOU THINK YOU'RE GOING TO BE SIX ALL YOUR LIFE.

# Calvin and Hobbes by WATERSON

AH·CHOO!

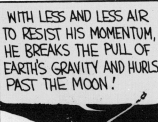

*WHEN* ... NO BRAINS.

AH.. AH.. AH.. **AH**

CHOOO!!

THE FORCE OF THE NASAL EXPLOSION SENDS CALVIN REELING THROUGH THE STRATOSPHERE!

WITH LESS AND LESS AIR TO RESIST HIS MOMENTUM, HE BREAKS THE PULL OF EARTH'S GRAVITY AND HURLS PAST THE MOON!

AS HE PASSES OUT OF THE GALAXY, CALVIN REFLECTS ON THE WISDOM OF COVERING ONE'S MOUTH WHEN SNEEZING TO DEFLECT THE PROPULSION.

ALAS, IT IS KNOWLEDGE GAINED TOO LATE FOR POOR CALVIN, THE HUMAN SATELLITE! ...BUT WAIT! ANOTHER SNEEZE IS BREWING! CALVIN TURNS HIMSELF AROUND!

THE SECOND SNEEZE ROCKETS HIM BACK TO EARTH! HE'S SAVED! IT'S A MIRACLE!

AH CHOO!

GOD BLESS YOU.

OH, HE *DOES*, MOM. HE *DOES*.

WATERSON

29

# calvin and hobbes

by WATTERSON

31

# Calvin and Hobbes

by WATTERSON

WIPE THAT GRIN OFF YOUR FACE!

WELL, HOBBES, HOW DO I LOOK?

I'M DOING MY BEST TO BITE MY TONGUE.

I CUT OUT CONSTRUCTION PAPER FEATHERS AND TAPED THEM ON MY ARMS SO I CAN FLY! PRETTY NEAT, HUH?

IF PAPER FEATHERS ARE ALL IT TAKES TO FLY, DON'T YOU THINK WE'D HAVE HEARD ABOUT IT BEFORE?

IT TAKES AN UNCOMMON MIND TO THINK OF THESE THINGS, HOBBES.

I'D AGREE WITH THAT.

HERE'S A GORGE. THIS IS A GOOD SPOT.

YOU'RE GOING TO JUMP OFF THIS LEDGE?

HECK NO! I NEED *MOMENTUM!* I WANT YOU TO *TOSS* ME OVER.

YOU UNDERSTAND I ASSUME NO RESPONSIBILITY FOR THIS?

RIGHT. *I* GET THE PATENT.

HEAVE!

I'M FLYING! I'M FLYING!

I'M..... UH OH...

DON'T SELL THE BIKE SHOP, ORVILLE.

SHUT UP AND GO GET ME SOME ANTISEPTIC.

# Calvin and Hobbes by WATTERSON

# Calvin and Hobbes

by WATTERSON

# CALVIN and HOBBES by WATERSON

First there was nothing...

...then there was Calvin!

Calvin, the mighty god, creates the universe with pure will!

From utter nothingness comes swirling form! Life begins where once was void!

But Calvin is no kind and loving god! He's one of the old gods! He demands sacrifice!

Yes, Calvin is a god of the underworld! And the puny inhabitants of earth displease him!

The great Calvin ignores their pleas for mercy and the doomed writhe in agony!

HAVE YOU SEEN HOW ABSORBED CALVIN IS WITH THOSE TINKERTOYS? HE'S CREATING WHOLE WORLDS OVER THERE!

I'LL BET HE GROWS UP TO BE AN ARCHITECT.

# CALVIN and HOBBES

by WATTERSON

HERE'S A BOX OF CRAYONS. I NEED SOME ILLUSTRATIONS FOR A STORY I'M WRITING.

---

YOU CAN DRAW SOMETHING BESIDES TIGERS, CAN'T YOU?

SURE. LEOPARDS, PUMAS, OCELOTS.. ..YOU NAME IT.

HERE, DAD, READ *THIS* STORY TONIGHT. I WROTE IT AND HOBBES ILLUSTRATED IT.

..UM... OK.

---

"THE DAD WHO LIVED TO REGRET BEING MEAN TO HIS KID."

WHAT ARE YOU PAUSING FOR? KEEP READING.

Barney's dad was really bad,
So Barney hatched a plan.
When his dad said, "Eat your peas!"
Barney shouted, "NO!" and ran.

peas

Barney

Barney tricked his mean ol' dad,
And locked him in the cellar.
His mom never found out
    where he'd gone,
'Cause Barney didn't tell her.

door

key

---

There his dad spent his life,
Eating mice and gruel.
With every bite for fifty years
He was sorry he'd been cruel.
        THE END.

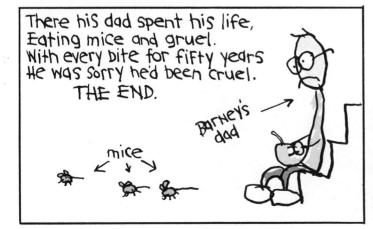

Barney's dad

mice

YOU KNOW HOW A LOT OF STORIES HAVE MORALS TO THEM...?

I *GET* IT, I *GET* IT!

WATTERSON & HOBS

45

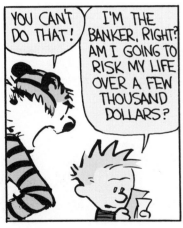

PLANET BOG — POOLS OF TOXIC CHEMICALS BUBBLE UNDER A CHOKING ATMOSPHERE OF POISONOUS GASES.

...BUT ASIDE FROM THAT, IT'S NOT MUCH LIKE EARTH.

WE FIND SPACEMAN SPIFF STRUGGLING ACROSS THE TERRAIN OF A DISTANT PLANET!

SUDDENLY THE GROUND BEGINS TO SHAKE! A CLOUD OF DUST APPEARS ON THE HORIZON! IT'S A ZORG!!

OUR HERO RUNS FOR COVER, BUT THE ZORG IS INSTANTLY UPON HIM!

SPIFF FIRES HIS BLASTER, BUT THE WEAPON IS USELESS AGAINST THE MONSTER!

THE FEARLESS SPACE EXPLORER IS TAKEN TO THE ZORG'S CAVE, WHERE HE DISCOVERS A VAT OF BOILING WATER! OH NO! OUR HERO IS ABOUT TO BE COOKED ALIVE!

SPIFF'S MIND RACES FURIOUSLY...

WELL? GET IN.

DON'T YOU WANT TO LEAN WAY, WAY OVER, AND TEST HOW HOT THE WATER IS?

50

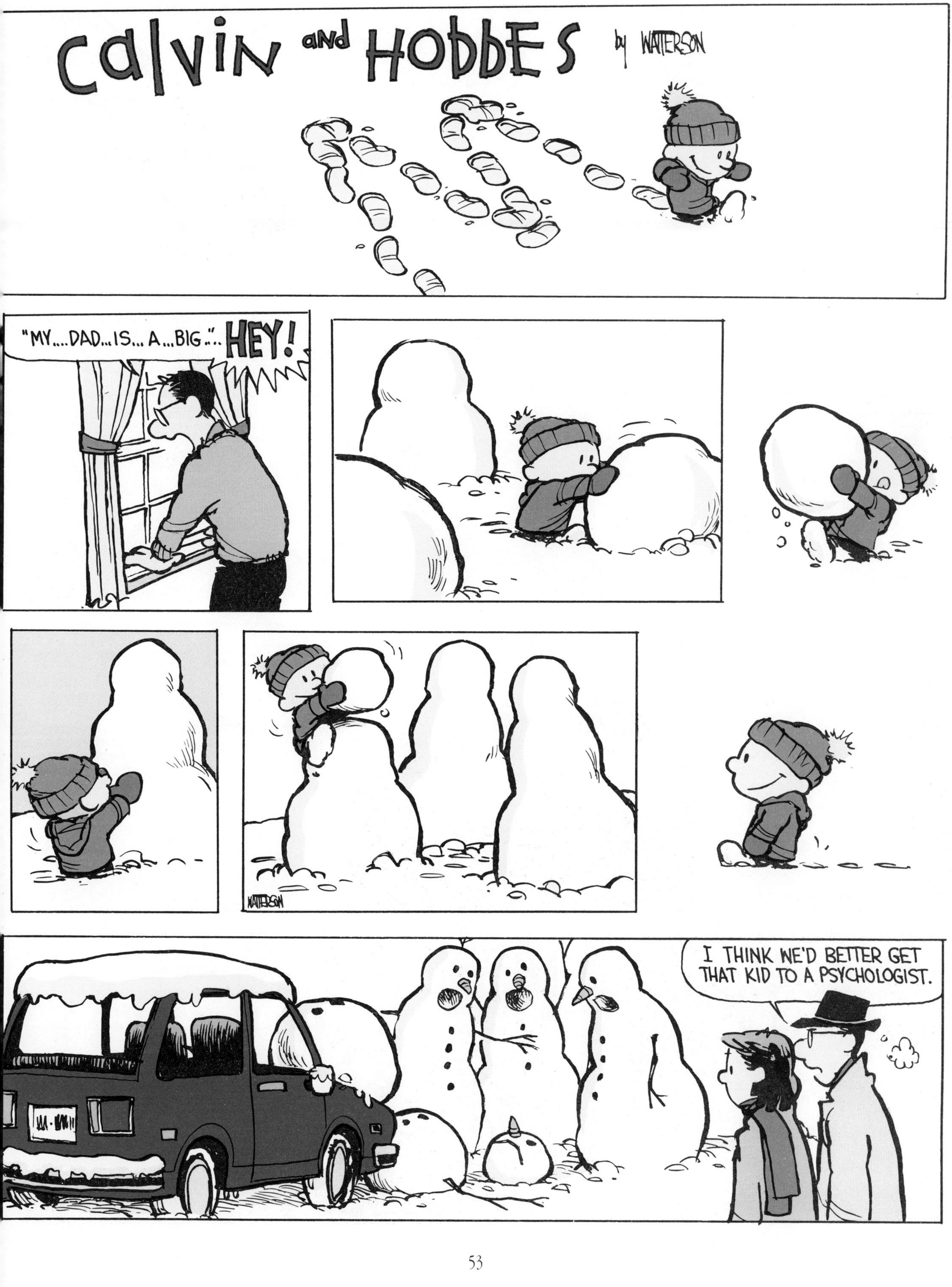

Calvin and HOBBES
by WATTERSON
"MY....DAD...IS... A...BIG...". HEY!
WATTERSON
I THINK WE'D BETTER GET THAT KID TO A PSYCHOLOGIST.

# Calvin and Hobbes

by WATTERSON

IT'S FREEZING UPSTAIRS!

CAN I TAKE SOME LOGS UP TO MY ROOM?

HEY, YOU'RE ON MY SIDE OF THE BED.

THESE SHEETS ARE FREEZING!

YEAH, WELL... AAUGHH! YOUR FEET ARE LIKE ICE! GET AWAY FROM ME!

BUT MY SIDE'S ALL COLD!

WELL DON'T GET ME COLD! MOVE OVER!

SURE, YOU'VE GOT A FUR COAT! I'M JUST WEARING PAJAMAS.

QUIT PULLING THE BLANKETS, WILLYA?

I HARDLY HAVE ANY, YOU HOG! GIMME THOSE!

YOU'RE LETTING IN COLD AIR! QUIT IT! QUIT IT!

SERVES YOU RIGHT, MR. MOSTY-TOASTY! SEE WHAT IT'S LIKE BEING COLD!

YAHHAH!!

EAT FEATHERS, FUZZ BALL!

WHAP OOF POW

MOVE OVER. YOU'RE GETTING MY SIDE ALL HOT.

OPEN THE WINDOW. I'M ROASTING.

54

# Calvin and Hobbes

by WATTERSON

THE LATE CRETACEOUS PERIOD... WHEN DINOSAURS RULED THE EARTH!

..AND CALVIN RULED THE DINOSAURS!

THE TERRIBLE TYRANNOSAURUS SINKS ITS TEETH INTO A TRICERATOPS!

TRIUMPHANT AGAIN, THE UNDISPUTED KING OF DINOSAURS LETS OUT A MIGHTY ROAR!

WITH SAVAGE FEROCITY, THE MONSTER BEGINS ITS FEAST! LIMB-SEVERING, BONE-CRUNCHING AND TENDON-SNAPPING, HE...

CALVIN! THAT'S DISGUSTING!

FOR HEAVEN'S SAKE, SLOW DOWN AND CHEW QUIETLY!

THE TERRIBLE TYRANNOSAURUS RESUMES EATING, MORTIFIED THAT SOMEONE MIGHT SEE HIM.

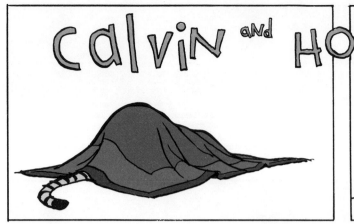

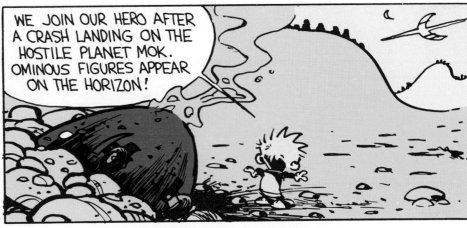

**CALVIN and HOBBES** by WATTERSON

YES, YOU CAN CERTAINLY SEE FAR FROM UP HERE.

I CALL THIS "LOOKOUT" HILL.

I CALL IT "LOOKOUT" HILL BECAUSE THAT'S WHAT YOU YELL WHENEVER WE GO DOWN IT.

YOU KNOW, SOMETIMES IT SEEMS THINGS GO BY TOO QUICKLY.

WE'RE SO BUSY WATCHING OUT FOR WHAT'S JUST AHEAD OF US THAT WE DON'T TAKE THE TIME TO ENJOY WHERE WE ARE.

DAYS GO BY AND WE HARDLY NOTICE THEM. LIFE BECOMES A BLUR.

OFTEN IT TAKES SOME CALAMITY TO MAKE US LIVE IN THE PRESENT.

THEN SUDDENLY WE WAKE UP AND SEE ALL THE MISTAKES WE'VE MADE, BUT IT'S TOO LATE TO CHANGE ANYTHING.

IT'S LIKE... ..IT'S LIKE...

IT'S LIKE WHAT?

IT'S LIKE *SOME*THING... I JUST CAN'T THINK OF IT.

# Calvin and Hobbes
## by WATTERSON

C'MON, HOBBES. LET ME UP INTO THE TREE FORT.

SAY THE PASSWORD.

NO! YOU KNOW IT'S ME! LET ME UP!

YOU MAY BE SOME OTHER KID IN DISGUISE.

IT'S *ME*, CALVIN! LET ME UP, YOU HAIRBALL BARFER!

AN INSULT! WELL, YOU CAN JUST STAY DOWN THERE *FOREVER*, MR. STINKER.

OH, NO! HERE COMES SUSIE! LET ME UP QUICK, SO WE CAN THROW THINGS AT HER! HURRY! LET DOWN THE ROPE!

LA DE DA DUM DOO ♪ ♫

SHE'S COMING! QUICK! LET DOWN THE ROPE! I'M SORRY I INSULTED YOU! OK? SEE, I SAID I WAS SORRY! CAN'T YOU LET DOWN THE ROPE?!

YOU HAVE TO SAY THE PASSWORD.

..Verse Seven:
TIGERS ARE PERFECT, THE *E*-PIT-O-ME OF GOOD LOOKS AND GRACE AND QUIET..UH..UM..DIGNITY.

I WAS GOING TO ASK YOU TO COME OVER AND PLAY HOUSE, BUT I THINK YOU'D BE A WEIRD EXAMPLE FOR OUR CHILDREN.

ONE OF THESE DAYS I'M GOING TO MAKE YOU INTO A RUG! YOU HEAR ME?? A RUG!

# Calvin and Hobbes

by WATTERSON

THE CALL GOES OUT! WE'RE ON THE MOVE!

UP THROUGH THE WINDING MAZE! FASTER! FASTER!

CALVIN SCRAMBLES UP THE GRAINY TUNNEL!

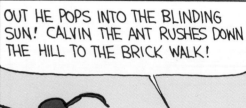

OUT HE POPS INTO THE BLINDING SUN! CALVIN THE ANT RUSHES DOWN THE HILL TO THE BRICK WALK!

OTHER ANTS RUSH AROUND HIM IN THEIR MAD HURRY! CALVIN TRIES TO KEEP UP!

AT LAST HE REACHES THE MONSTROUS DEAD CATERPILLAR! WITHOUT PAUSING, HE HOISTS IT UP!

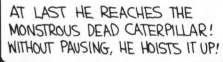

THE QUEEN DEMANDS HIS TIRELESS TOIL! CALVIN IS BACK OFF TO THE ANT-HILL AS FAST AS HE CAN GO!

WORK, WORK, WORK! THAT'S ALL I'M GOOD FOR AROUND HERE!

I HARDLY THINK PICKING UP YOUR ROOM ONCE IN A WHILE QUALIFIES YOU AS A SLAVE.

WATTERSON

# Calvin and Hobbes

by WATTERSON

THIS IS CALVIN, YOUR CAPTAIN, SPEAKING...

...JUST TO REASSURE YOU THAT, YES, THERE IS SOMEONE UP FRONT.

CALVIN PILOTS THE JET AIRLINER ACROSS THE COUNTRY AT 35,000 FEET.

HE IS GIVEN CLEARANCE TO LAND. BUT WHAT'S THIS? A PLANE FROM A RIVAL AIRLINE IS MAKING FOR THE SAME RUNWAY TO SHAVE PRECIOUS MINUTES OFF ITS SCHEDULE!

WATTERSON

IT'S A 600·MPH GAME OF CHICKEN! CALVIN PULLS BACK ON THE THROTTLE AND LURCHES AHEAD!

THE OTHER PILOT TRIES TO CUT CALVIN OFF WITH A SUDDEN DROP IN ALTITUDE!

CALVIN SWITCHES ON THE "FASTEN SEAT BELT" LIGHT IN THE CABIN, AND DOES A BARREL ROLL!

AT 5 Gs, CALVIN HOPES NOT TO BLACK OUT!

AS THEY CLOSE IN ON THE RUNWAY, THE OTHER PILOT HAS NO CHOICE BUT TO PULL UP AND CIRCLE AROUND AGAIN! CALVIN WINS!

HEY, MOM, IS IT TRUE I COULD GET A PILOT'S LICENSE AT AGE 14?

NO.

# CALViN aNd HObbEs by WATERSON

zzzzzzzzzzzzz

FILTH! CONTAMINATION! PESTILENCE! HA HA HA!

OF ALL LIVING CREATURES, FEW ARE MORE REPULSIVE THAN CALVIN THE BUG!

HE EXISTS ONLY TO SUCK BLOOD AND TRANSMIT PARASITIC DISEASE!

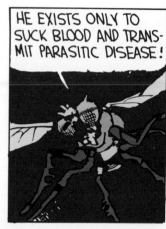

SEARCHING FOR SOMEONE TO INFECT, CALVIN FLIES LOW OVER THE PICNIC TABLE!

INGREDIENTS: SALT,

HIS SENSITIVE ANTENNAE PICK UP THE SCENT OF HUMAN FLESH!

TOUCHING DOWN, CALVIN INSERTS HIS NEEDLELIKE PROBOSCIS INTO A VEIN! PROTOZOANS IN HIS SALIVA QUICKLY INDUCE PLAGUE!

WILL YOU STOP THAT AWFUL SLURPING?! YOU'RE MAKING ME SICK!

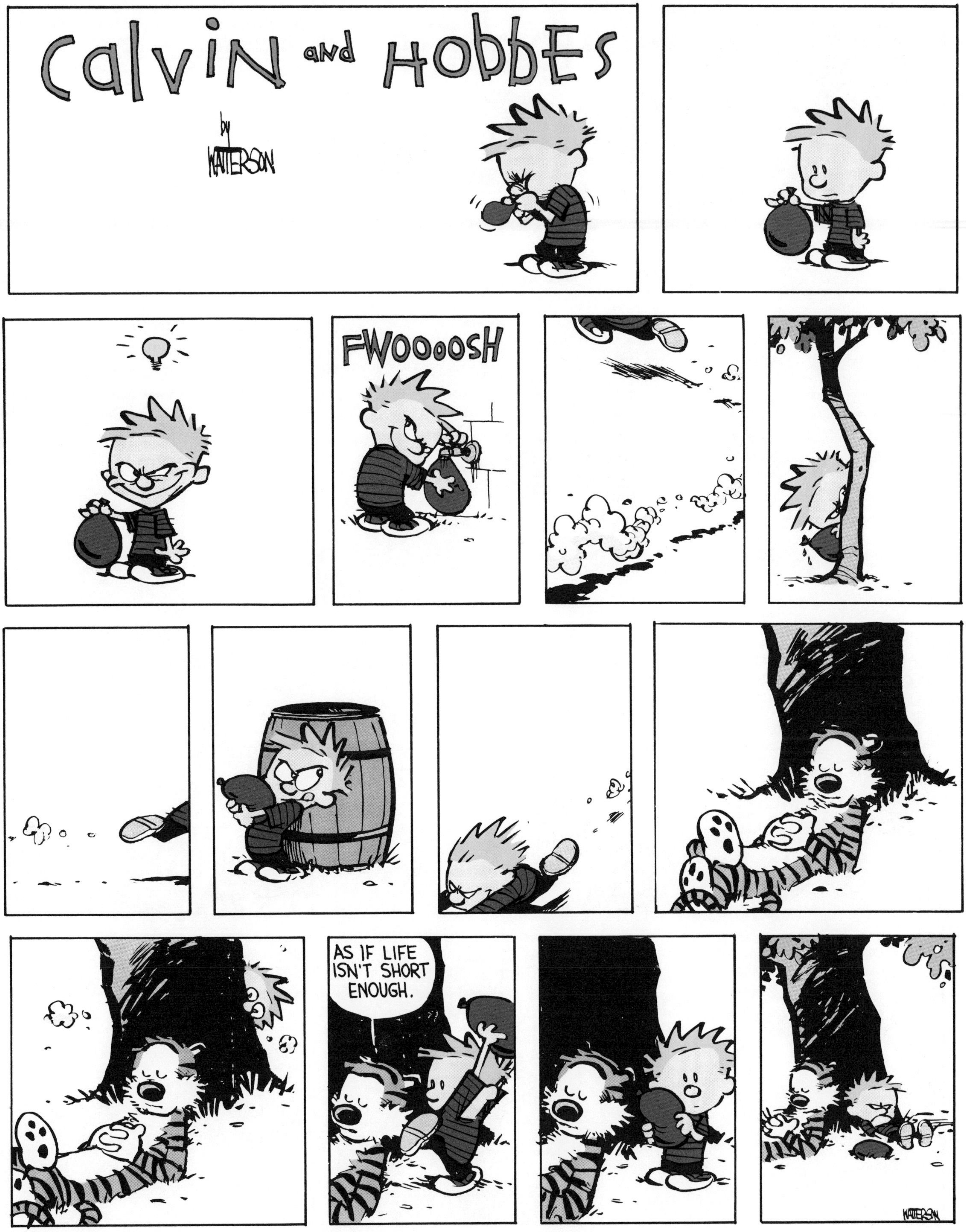
Calvin and HOBBES
by WATTERSON
FWOOOOOSH
AS IF LIFE ISN'T SHORT ENOUGH.
WATTERSON

68

# Calvin and Hobbes

by WATTERSON

SPACEMAN SPIFF EXPLORES THE OUTERMOST REACHES OF THE UNIVERSE.

BY POPULAR REQUEST.

INTREPID EXPLORER SPACEMAN SPIFF LANDS ON AN UNCHARTED PLANET. WHAT STRANGE WONDERS WILL HE DISCOVER HERE?

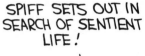

SPIFF SETS OUT IN SEARCH OF SENTIENT LIFE!

WHAT A STRANGE PLANET THIS IS! ITS SURFACE IS SURPRISINGLY SOFT AND POROUS!

AND HERE CURIOUS GEYSERS BLAST HOT AIR!

SUDDENLY IT DAWNS ON HIM! SPIFF IS NOT ON THE PLANET'S SURFACE AT ALL! HE'S WALKING ON A RECLINING ALIEN!!

OUR HERO SETS HIS DEATH RAY BLASTER.

ZZ.. MMF HM?

71

# Calvin and Hobbes
## by WATTERSON

HERE'S "HAMSTER HUEY AND THE GOOEY KABLOOIE." YOU MIGHT LIKE THIS STORY.

YEAH? HOW GOOD CAN IT BE IF IT HASN'T BEEN MADE INTO AN ANIMATED TV SHOW?

I HOPE TONIGHT'S STORY ISN'T AS BORING AS *LAST* NIGHT'S WAS. IT PUT ME RIGHT TO SLEEP.

DON'T WORRY. *THIS* STORY WILL KEEP YOU UP ALL NIGHT.

REALLY? WHAT IS IT?

IT'S CALLED, "THE DISEMBODIED HAND THAT STRANGLED PEOPLE."

GOSH, THIS IS GREAT! HOW CREEPY! I *NEVER* GET A SCARY STORY! A DISEMBODIED HAND! WOW!

AND YOU KNOW WHAT'S *REALLY* SCARY? THEY NEVER FOUND IT! TO THIS DAY, NOBODY KNOWS WHERE THE HAND IS!

WATTERSON

IN FACT, THE HAND COULD... OH NO!! THERE IT IS!

IT'S G-GOT ME!! GAKK!!

..CALVIN?.. ..CALVIN?..

I SHOULD'VE THOUGHT OF THAT YEARS AGO.

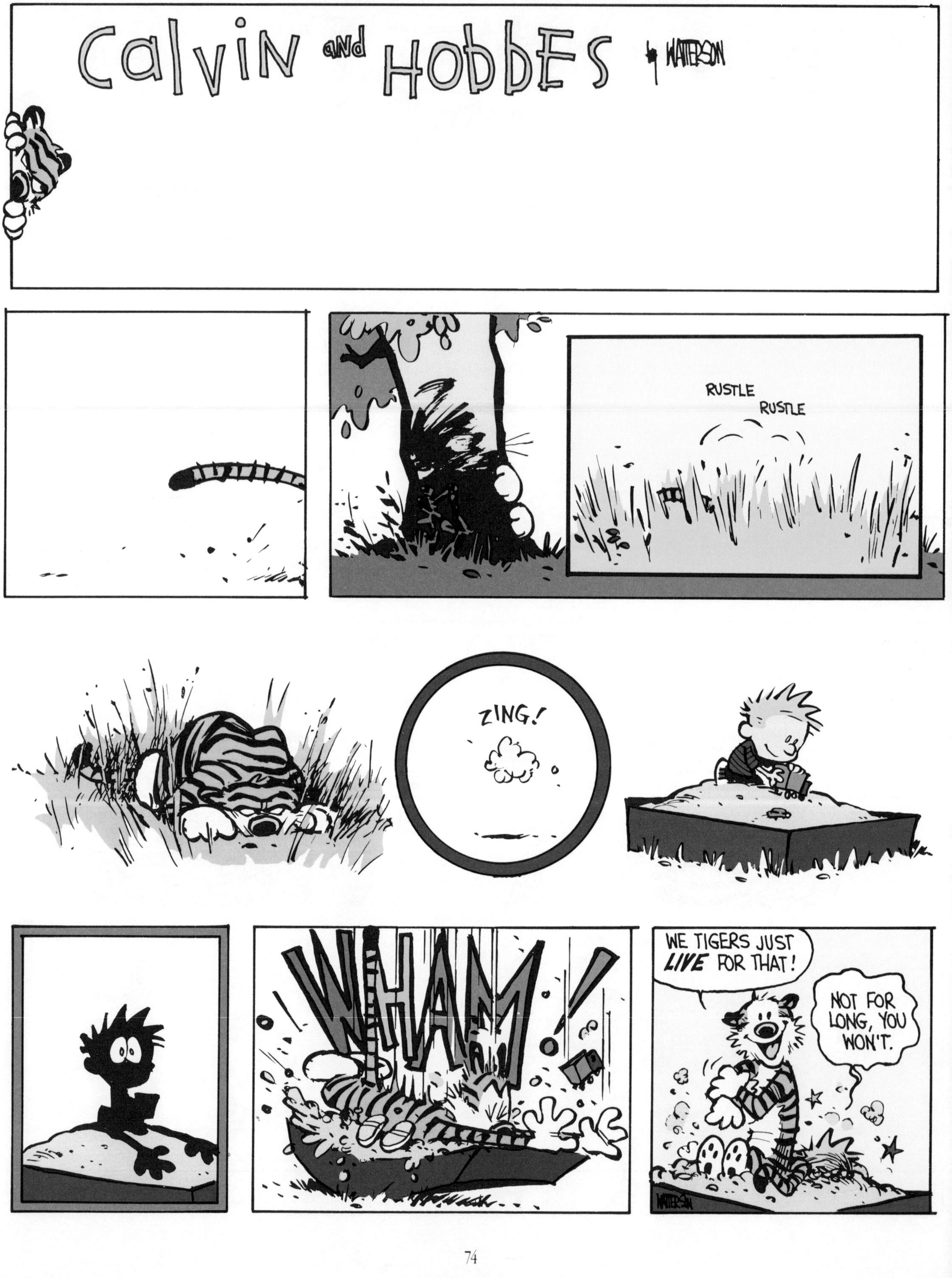
Calvin and HOBBES by WATTERSON
RUSTLE
RUSTLE
ZING!
WHAM!
WE TIGERS JUST LIVE FOR THAT!
NOT FOR LONG, YOU WON'T.
WATTERSON

# Calvin and Hobbes

by WATTERSON

WOW! HOW DID YOU EVER GET SO MUDDY?!

WELL, I WAS JUST STANDING THERE, MINDING MY OWN BUSINESS, WHEN ALL OF A SUDDEN, A HORDE OF DIRTY CANNIBALS COMES...

FORGET IT.

BOY, WHAT A DELIGHTFUL AFTERNOON.

SOMETIMES I FEEL LIKE I WORK ALL THE TIME TO AFFORD THIS PLACE, AND I NEVER GET TO SIT BACK WITH A GOOD BOOK AND ENJOY IT.

WELL, AT LEAST I HAVE THE WEEKENDS TO...

CALVIN

YOU GOT MUD ALL OVER THE HOUSE! LOOK AT YOU! AIEE~THE COUCH! WHAT'D YOU DO?! DID YOU WALK ACROSS THE COUCH?!

I DIDN'T DO IT! SOMEONE ELSE MUST HAVE! I JUST SAW A MUDDY GUY GO RUNNING FROM...

OUT! OUT OF THE HOUSE! NOW!

OK, OK! I'M GOING! YOU DON'T NEED TO PUSH! I CAN TELL WHEN I'M NOT WANTED! HEY! LEGGO! OW! ALL RIGHT, GOODBYE!

HEY, DAD, CATCH THE WATER BALLOON!

GREAT REFLEXES, DAD. BY THE WAY, DON'T GO IN THE HOUSE LIKE THAT. MOM'S IN ONE OF HER MOODS AGAIN.

I'LL BET I COULD GET A LOT OF WORK DONE AT THE OFFICE ON WEEKENDS...

WATTERSON

76

# Calvin and Hobbes

by WATTERSON

SCHOOL'S OUT! FREE AT LAST!

AND JUST SIX PRECIOUS HOURS BEFORE BED TO FORGET EVERYTHING I LEARNED TODAY.

I HATE COMING HOME FROM SCHOOL. I NEVER KNOW IF HOBBES IS WAITING TO POUNCE ON ME.

MAYBE I CAN STAND OFF TO THE SIDE HERE, AND PUSH THE DOOR OPEN WITH A STICK.

I'M HOME!

KAPOW!

WHAT DO YOU DO, WAIT UNTIL YOU SEE THE WHITES OF MY EYES?!?

BOY, YOU SHOULD'VE SEEN THEM! THEY WERE AS BIG AS DINNER PLATES! HOO HOO HOO!

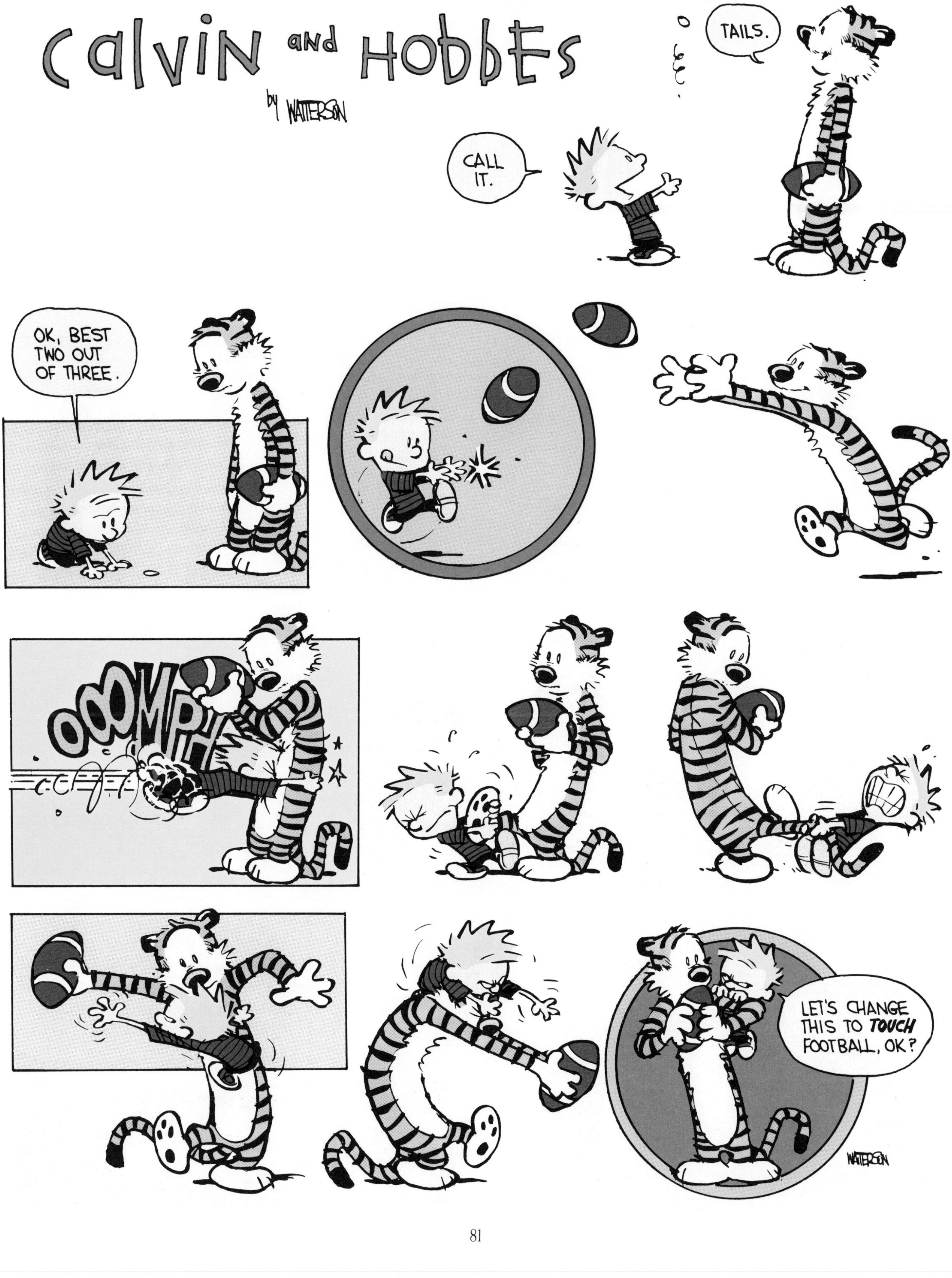
Calvin and HOBBES
by WATTERSON
CALL IT.
TAILS.
OK, BEST TWO OUT OF THREE.
OOOMPH
LET'S CHANGE THIS TO **TOUCH** FOOTBALL, OK?
WATTERSON

# CALVIN and HOBBES

by WATTERSON

UH-OH.

SOMETHING IS VERY WRONG HERE.

CALVIN HAS MYSTERIOUSLY SHRUNK TO A QUARTER OF AN INCH TALL!

HOW CAN HE MAKE HIS PLIGHT KNOWN TO HIS PARENTS WHEN HE'S SMALLER THAN A PENNY?

CALVIN GETS AN IDEA! HE GRABS THE LEG OF OF A PASSING HOUSEFLY AND FLIES TO HIS DAD'S CAMERA!

ONCE THERE, HE CLIMBS UP AND SETS THE SELF-TIMER.

JUMPING ON THE SHUTTER, CALVIN HAS FIFTEEN SHORT SECONDS TO GET IN FRONT OF THE LENS!

WITH LUCK, CALVIN'S DAD WILL HAVE THE FILM DEVELOPED SOON, AND DISCOVER WHAT HAS HAPPENED!

WHAT HAPPENED?! LOOK AT ALL THESE TERRIBLE PICTURES! I DON'T REMEMBER TAKING THESE. WHO'S THAT LITTLE SPECK IN THE DISTANCE ALL THE TIME? YOU HAVEN'T BEEN FOOLING WITH MY CAMERA, HAVE YOU?

ME? HECK, NO. MAYBE YOU SHOULD GET THE CAMERA FIXED.

# Calvin and Hobbes

### by WATTERSON

THE VALIANT SPACEMAN SPIFF, INTERGALACTIC EXPLORER, COMES IN OVER THE MOUNTAINS OF A STRANGE PLANET!

OUR HERO DESPERATELY HOPES TO FIND A REST AREA WITH WORKING FACILITIES.

SPACEMAN SPIFF LANDS ON THE DISTANT PLANET ZOKK!

CLIMBING DOWN FROM HIS SPACECRAFT, OUR HERO PREPARES TO EXPLORE THE SURFACE!

UNEXPECTEDLY, SPIFF'S FIRST STEP SENDS HIM CAREENING THROUGH THE SKY!

SPIFF QUICKLY REALIZES THAT PLANET ZOKK HAS ONLY A FRACTION OF EARTH'S GRAVITY!

OOF

WITH PRACTICE, OUR HERO SOON FINDS HE CAN BOUND EFFORTLESSLY ACROSS THE LANDSCAPE!

WATTERSON

STOP BOUNCING ON THE BED AND GO TO SLEEP!

# Calvin and Hobbes

by WATTERSON

89

# Calvin and Hobbes

by Watterson

90

# Calvin and Hobbes

by WATTERSON

IF *I* WAS IN CHARGE, WE'D NEVER SEE GRASS BETWEEN OCTOBER AND MAY.

ON "THREE," READY? ONE... TWO... THREE!

SNOW!

I SAID SNOW! C'MON! SNOW!

SNOW!

OK THEN, *DON'T* SNOW! SEE WHAT *I* CARE! I *LIKE* THIS WEATHER! LET'S HAVE IT FOREVER!

*PLEEAASE* SNOW! PLEASE?? JUST A FOOT! OK, EIGHT INCHES! THAT'S ALL! C'MON! SIX INCHES, EVEN! HOW ABOUT JUST SIX??

I'M *WAAIIITING...*

RRRRGGGHHH

DO YOU WANT ME TO BECOME AN ATHEIST?

# CALVIN and HOBBES — by WATTERSON

WHO **IS** THIS MYSTERIOUS MASKED MAN??

KAPWIINGG!

AND WHY HAS HE NEVER BEEN PHOTOGRAPHED TOGETHER WITH HANDSOME, 6-YEAR-OLD MILLIONAIRE PLAYBOY CALVIN?

A SOLITARY CAPED FIGURE RUNS ACROSS A MOONLIT BUILDING TOP!

A CRIMSON BOLT BLASTS ACROSS THE NIGHT SKY, STRIKING FEAR INTO THE HEARTS OF ALL EVILDOERS!

YES, IT'S *STUPENDOUS MAN*, CHAMPION OF LIBERTY, DEFENDER OF FREE WILL!

SOME DIABOLICAL FIEND THREATENS TO ESTABLISH A TOTALITARIAN SYSTEM OF RULE! ONLY *STUPENDOUS MAN* CAN SAVE THE DAY!

AHA! JUST AS I SUSPECTED! MY EVIL ARCHNEMESIS, *MOM-LADY*!

DIDN'T I TELL YOU TO GO TO BED?!?

OH, NO! STUPENDOUS MAN'S STUPENDOUS POWERS ARE NO MATCH AGAINST HIS ADVERSARY! STUPENDOUS MAN IS VANQUISHED!

THIS WOULD HAVE BEEN PLENTY HUMILIATING *WITHOUT* THE GOODNIGHT KISS.

AND TAKE OFF THAT SILLY HOOD BEFORE YOU SMOTHER IN YOUR SLEEP.

# CALVIN and HOBBES
by WATTERSON

AHH... THE PERFECT SLUSHBALL!

HARD ENOUGH TO STING, YET SLOPPY ENOUGH TO DRIBBLE DOWN THE COLLAR AND SOAK THE UNDERGARMENTS.

HERE COMES SUSIE! NOW'S MY CHANCE TO HIT HER WITH A SLUSHBALL!

I SEE YOU! YOU'D BETTER NOT THROW THAT! SANTA CLAUS IS WATCHING YOU RIGHT NOW!

FWISSHHH!

ZINGG

WHAP!

OH YES! YES! IT WAS WORTH IT! WHAT A SHOT! I'M NOT SORRY! OH, IT WAS BEAUTIFUL! I'D DO IT AGAIN IN A MINUTE! HA HA!

SANTA'S GONNA SKIP THIS BLOCK FOR YEARS.

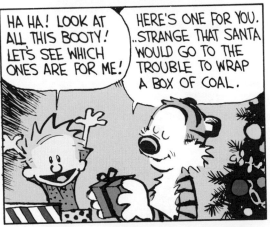

OK, LET'S SEE... IF THE WIND IS BLOWING NORTH-NORTHEAST AT 6 MPH, AND I THROW THE SNOWBALL DUE WEST AT 90 MPH WITH A SLIGHT TOP SPIN ....

HA! SUSIE DIDN'T EVEN HEAR ME SNEAK UP!

NOW I'LL CREAM HER CRANIUM WITH A BARRAGE OF SNOWBALLS!

WHIZZZ

PIFF

PIFF

THESE DARN CROSS BREEZES! SHE DIDN'T EVEN NOTICE!

YOU'RE THE WORST SHOT IN THE WORLD, CALVIN! IF IT WASN'T FOR GRAVITY, YOU PROBABLY COULDN'T EVEN HIT THE GROUND!

SMACK!

I DID IT! I DID IT! JUST WHEN IT REALLY COUNTED, I DID IT! HA HA HA! RIGHT IN THE KISSER! HA HA!

BAD NEWS, MOM. I PROMISED MY SOUL TO THE DEVIL THIS AFTERNOON.

OH? THAT RECENTLY?

# CalViN and HObbEs

by WATTERSON

# Calvin and Hobbes by WATTERSON

WHAT'S THIS?

A CALVIN DECOY. PRETTY GOOD, HUH?

NOW I CAN FIND OUT WHO MY ENEMIES ARE! I'LL HIDE BEHIND THAT TREE OVER THERE AND WATCH TO SEE WHO THROWS SNOWBALLS AT THE DECOY, THINKING IT'S ME!

YOUR ENEMIES MUST NOT BE VERY BRIGHT.

THAT'S WHY THEY'RE OUT TO GET ME. THEY CAN'T STAND MY GENIUS.

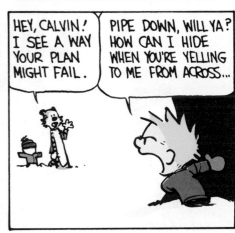

HEY, CALVIN! I SEE A WAY YOUR PLAN MIGHT FAIL.

PIPE DOWN, WILL YA? HOW CAN I HIDE WHEN YOU'RE YELLING TO ME FROM ACROSS...

SMACK!

SEE THERE? MY PLAN TO DISCOVER MY ENEMIES WAS A COMPLETE SUCCESS.

TOO BAD YOU TOOK OFF YOUR COAT AND HAT. YOU MUST BE SOAKED.

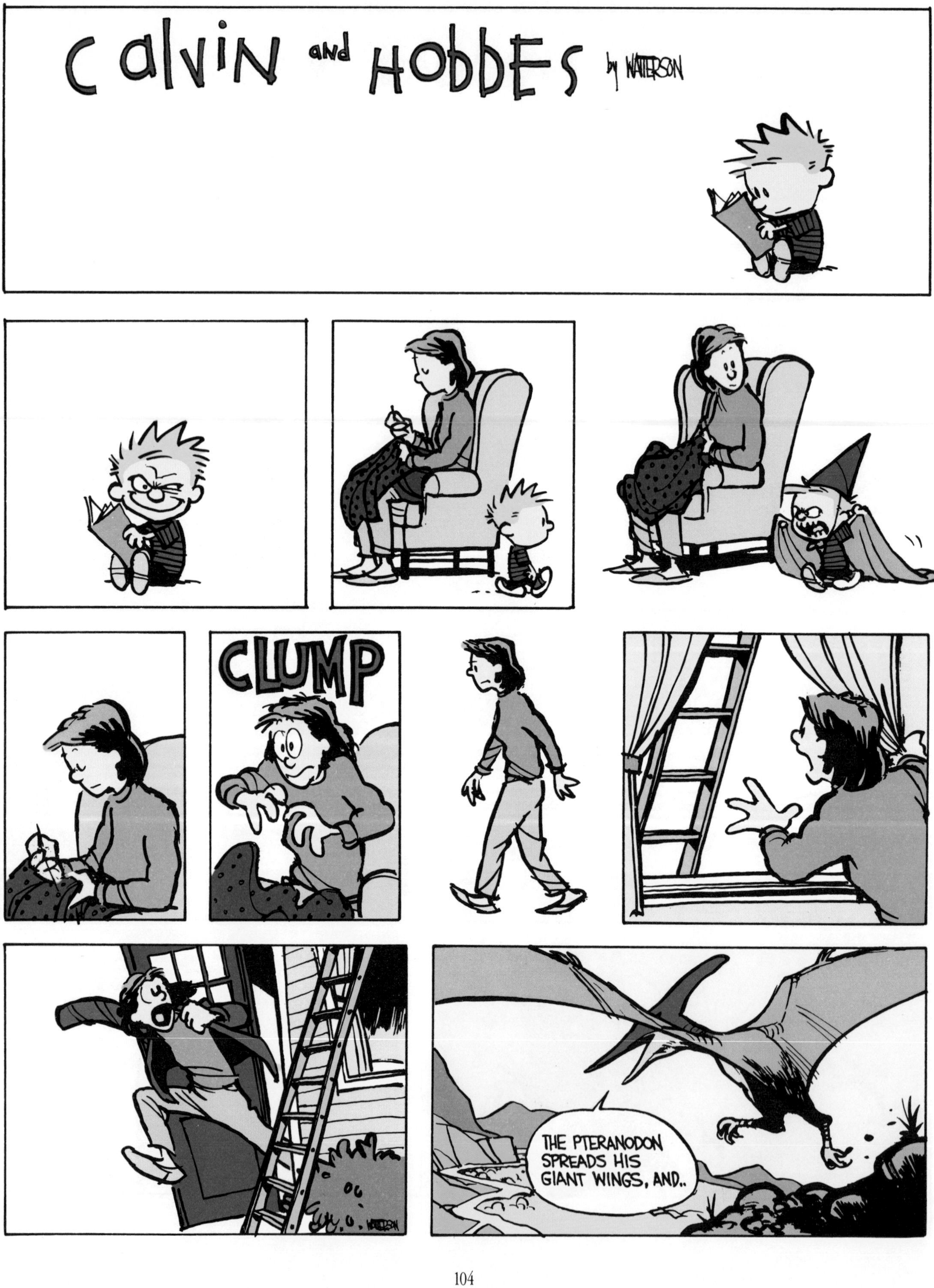
Calvin and HOBBES by WATTERSON
CLUMP
THE PTERANODON SPREADS HIS GIANT WINGS, AND..
WATTERSON

# calvin and Hobbes by Watterson

I CAN NEVER ENJOY SUNDAYS, BECAUSE IN THE BACK OF MY MIND I ALWAYS KNOW I'VE GOT TO GO TO SCHOOL THE NEXT DAY.

IT'S LIKE TRYING TO ENJOY YOUR LAST MEAL BEFORE THE EXECUTION.

A PENNY FOR YOUR THOUGHTS

SORRY. *MY* THOUGHTS ARE A BUCK APIECE.

A DOLLAR?! THAT'S OUTRAGEOUS! YOUR THOUGHTS AREN'T WORTH THAT!

*THIS* ONE IS! AT A DOLLAR, IT'S THE BAR-GAIN OF A LIFETIME.

I WOULDN'T PAY A NICKLE FOR ANY THOUGHT YOU'VE EVER HAD IN YOUR WHOLE FLEA-RIDDEN EXISTENCE!

THAT LITTLE REMARK JUST MADE THE PRICE *TEN* DOLLARS!

*TEN??* YOU CAN'T EXTORT ME! *KEEP* YOUR STUPID THOUGHT!

IF YOU KNEW WHAT IT WAS, YOU'D *BEG* TO PAY TEN BUCKS FOR IT.

C'MON, JUST TELL ME WHAT IT IS, WILL YOU?

NOTHING DOING, PAL.

OK, OK! I'LL GIVE YOU 25 CENTS. THAT'S ALL I HAVE.

LET'S SEE IT.

*HERE!* 25 CENTS! NOW WHAT'S THIS BIG, EXPENSIVE THOUGHT OF YOURS?!

"A FOOL AND HIS MONEY ARE SOON PAR..."

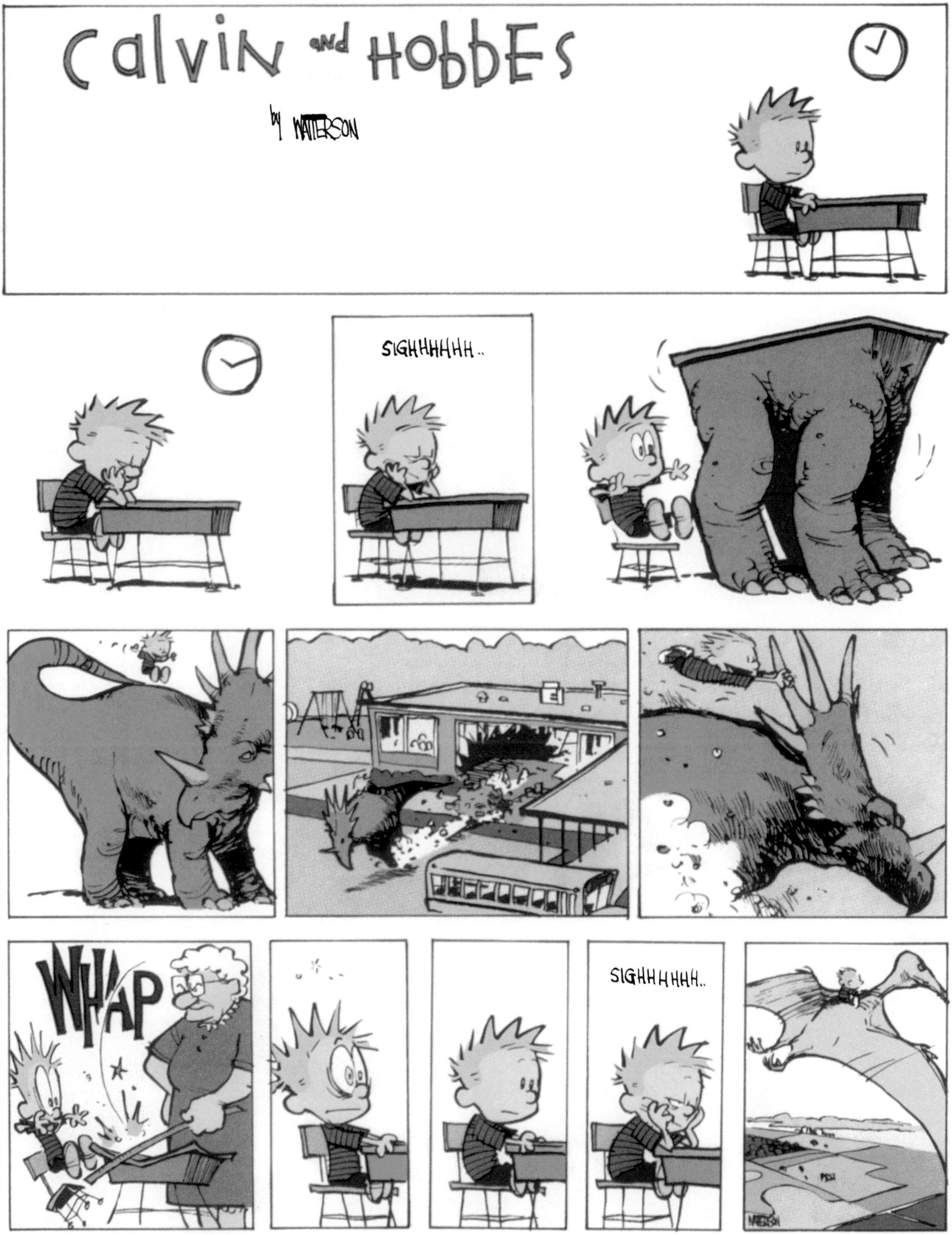
Calvin and HOBBES
by WATTERSON
SIGHHHHHH..
WHAP
SIGHHHHHH..

# CALVIN and HOBBES

by WATTERSON

GET UP, CALVIN! I'M NOT GOING TO CALL YOU AGAIN!

I BET.

YOU'RE GOING TO MISS THE BUS! NOW GET OUT OF BED!

YOU DON'T KNOW THE ANSWER? THEN SIT DOWN.

Hey, Twinky, want to see if there's an afterlife?

NO, YOU CAN'T GO PLAY UNTIL YOU FINISH YOUR HOMEWORK.

JUST EAT YOUR FOOD. YOU DON'T NEED TO PLAY WITH IT.

STOP STALLING AND GET IN THE BATHTUB.

NO, YOU CAN'T STAY UP A LITTLE LONGER. GO TO BED.

HAVE A GOOD NIGHT'S SLEEP. TOMORROW'S ANOTHER BIG DAY!

... SIGHHHHHH ...

# calvin and HOBBES
## by WATTERSON

THREE... TWO... ONE...

LIGHT SPEED!

BLASTING ACROSS THE GALAXY IN HYPER LIGHT DRIVE, IT'S *SPACEMAN SPIFF*, INTERPLANETARY EXPLORER EXTRAORDIN...

SINCE CALVIN SEEMS TO BE ENJOYING THE LESSON, LET'S HAVE HIM DEMONSTRATE THE NEXT PROBLEM.

*ZOUNDS!* A ZOK DEATH SLOOP APPEARS OUT OF NOWHERE AND FRIES SPIFF'S STABILIZERS!

OUR HERO HURLS OUT OF CONTROL TOWARD HIS IMMINENT DOOM!

THE SITUATION IS DESPERATE! THIS COULD BE THE END! WHAT CAN OUR HERO DO??

HIS MIND RACING FURIOUSLY, SPIFF SPRINGS INTO ACTION! HE DOWNSHIFTS HIS SPACECRAFT AND...

... STALLS.

RINGG!

OH, DARN, OUT OF TIME.

ONCE AGAIN SPACEMAN SPIFF BEATS ALL ODDS TO SAVE THE DAY!

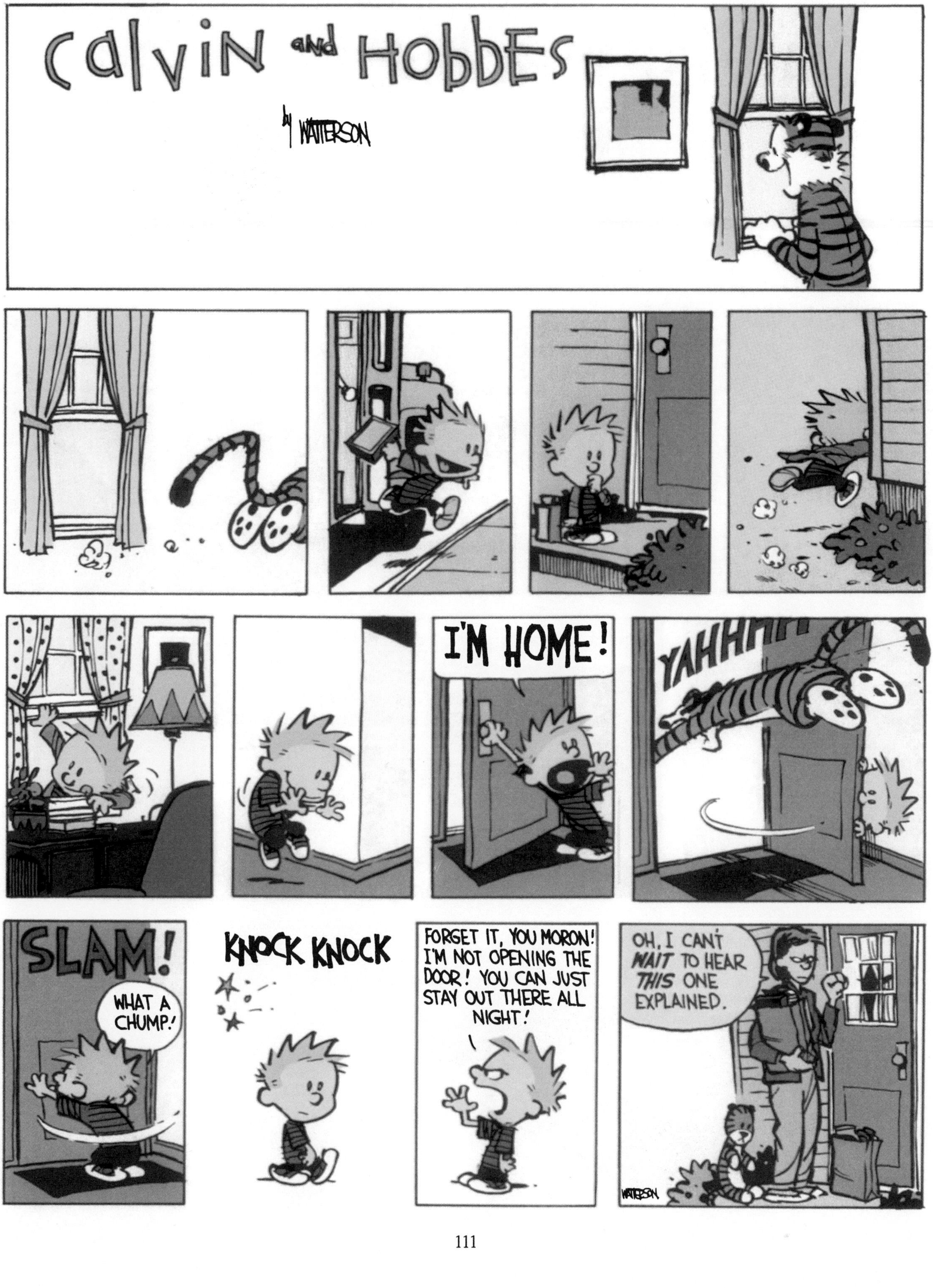
Calvin and HOBBES
by WATTERSON
I'M HOME!
YAHHHH
SLAM!
WHAT A CHUMP!
KNOCK KNOCK
FORGET IT, YOU MORON! I'M NOT OPENING THE DOOR! YOU CAN JUST STAY OUT THERE ALL NIGHT!
OH, I CAN'T WAIT TO HEAR THIS ONE EXPLAINED.
WATTERSON

# CALVIN and HOBBES
by WATTERSON

I CAN'T SLEEP.

I THINK NIGHTTIME IS DARK SO YOU CAN IMAGINE YOUR FEARS WITH LESS DISTRACTION.

AT NIGHTTIME, THE WORLD ALWAYS SEEMS SO BIG AND SCARY, AND I ALWAYS SEEM SO SMALL.

I WISH I COULD FALL ASLEEP, SO IT WOULD BE MORNING.

SIGHHHHH..

LOOK AT HOBBES. *HE'S* ASLEEP.

Z

HEH HEH... HE SURE LOOKS FUNNY WHEN HE SLEEPS. TIGERS CLOSE THEIR EYES SO TIGHT. I WONDER WHAT HE'S DREAMING ABOUT.

GOOD OL' HOBBES. WHAT A FRIEND.

Z

THINGS ARE NEVER QUITE AS SCARY WHEN YOU'VE GOT A BEST FRIEND.

Z

Z

Z    Z

# Calvin and Hobbes

by WATTERSON

TRUE FRIENDS ARE HARD TO COME BY.

I NEED MORE MONEY.

I WISH PEOPLE WERE MORE LIKE ANIMALS.

ANIMALS DON'T TRY TO CHANGE YOU OR MAKE YOU FIT IN. THEY JUST ENJOY THE PLEASURE OF YOUR COMPANY.

ANIMALS AREN'T CONDITIONAL ABOUT FRIENDSHIPS. ANIMALS LIKE YOU JUST THE WAY YOU ARE.

THEY LISTEN TO YOUR PROBLEMS, THEY COMFORT YOU WHEN YOU'RE SAD, AND ALL THEY ASK IN RETURN IS A LITTLE KINDNESS.

WHOOONK! *SOB* IT'S SO...SO *TRUE*! HOOOOT! THBPBTPTH.

WATTERSON

...AND SPEAKING OF "A LITTLE KINDNESS," I'D HAVE A TUNA FISH SANDWICH ANY TIME SOON THAT YOU HAPPEN TO MAKE ONE...

OF COURSE, *SOME* ANIMALS GET ON YOUR NERVES ONCE IN A WHILE.

# Calvin and Hobbes
by WATTERSON

MILD-MANNERED CALVIN IS STUCK INSIDE DOING MATH PROBLEMS ON A BEAUTIFUL SUNDAY.

NO ONE IS WATCHING! HE DASHES INTO HIS CLOSET! *THIS* IS A JOB FOR...

## STUPENDOUS MAN!
DEFENDER OF FREEDOM! ADVOCATE OF LIBERTY!

A BRIGHT CRIMSON STREAK BLASTS UP THROUGH THE ATMOSPHERE, AND THEN TURNS BACK TOWARD EARTH!

GAINING STUPENDOUS MOMENTUM, *STUPENDOUS MAN* STRIKES THE GROUND AT AN ACUTE ANGLE WITH STUPENDOUS FORCE!

THE EARTH SLOWLY STOPS ROTATING... AND BEGINS TO TURN IN THE OPPOSITE DIRECTION!

PUSHING WITH ALL HIS MIGHT, *STUPENDOUS MAN* TURNS THE PLANET ALL THE WAY AROUND BACKWARD! THE SUN SETS IN THE EAST AND RISES IN THE WEST! SOON IT'S 10 A.M. THE PREVIOUS DAY!

WHAT ARE YOU DOING OUTSIDE? DID YOU FINISH YOUR HOMEWORK ALREADY?

IT'S SATURDAY! I DON'T NEED TO DO IT UNTIL TOMORROW... THANKS TO *STUPENDOUS MAN!*

# CalViN aNd HobbEs

by WATTERSON

DEAR MOM,
HOW DO I LOVE YOU?
LET ME COUNT THE WAYS:

ONE.... NUMBER ONE .....HMM...
NUMMMBER ONE .... MM.....

HEY, MOM, WAKE UP! I MADE YOU A MOTHER'S DAY CARD!

WHY, HOW SWEET OF YOU!

I DID IT ALL BY MYSELF. GO AHEAD AND READ IT!

"I WAS GOING TO BUY A CARD WITH HEARTS OF PINK AND RED, BUT THEN I THOUGHT I'D RATHER SPEND THE MONEY ON ME, INSTEAD."

"IT'S AWFULLY HARD TO BUY THINGS WHEN ONE'S ALLOWANCE IS SO SMALL...

..AHEM..

...SO I GUESS YOU'RE PRETTY LUCKY I GOT YOU ANYTHING AT ALL."

"HAPPY MOTHER'S DAY TO YOU. THERE, I SAID IT. NOW I'M DONE. SO HOW 'BOUT GETTING OUT OF BED, AND COOKING BREAKFAST FOR YOUR SON?"

I'M DEEPLY MOVED.

DID YOU NOTICE THE PART ABOUT MY ALLOWANCE?

# caLViN and HObbEs

by WATTERSON

AHHHH...

UH-OH. SOMETHING IS SERIOUSLY WRONG HERE.

THE LAWS OF PERSPECTIVE HAVE BEEN REPEALED!

OBJECTS NO LONGER DIMINISH IN SIZE WITH DISTANCE!

LINES DO NOT CONVERGE TOWARD ANY POINT ON THE HORIZON!

ALL SPATIAL RELATIONSHIPS ARE LOST! IT'S IMPOSSIBLE TO JUDGE WHERE ANYTHING IS! OH NO!

CALVIN, QUIT RUNNING AROUND AND CRASHING INTO THINGS, OR I'LL SELL YOU TO THE MONKEY HOUSE!

...AND NOW *SHE'S* LOST PERSPECTIVE.

# CALVIN and HOBBES

by WATTERSON

YOU CAN TAKE THE TIGER OUT OF THE JUNGLE, BUT YOU CAN'T TAKE THE JUNGLE OUT OF THE TIGER!

THE QUESTION *IS*, HOW CAN YOU GET THE TIGER *BACK* IN THE JUNGLE?

# Calvin and Hobbes

by WATTERSON

DO RE MI FA SO LA TI DO

A SPARROW ALIGHTS UPON A TREE BRANCH.

BUT THIS IS NO *ORDINARY* SPARROW! THIS IS A *SONG* SPARROW!

SWAYING GENTLY IN THE BREEZE, HE PREPARES TO BURST FORTH IN RAPTUROUS MELODY!

ON TOP OF SPA-GHETTI

ALL COVERED WITH CHEEEESE, I LOST MY POOR MEEEATBALLL, WHEN...

# Calvin and Hobbes
by WATTERSON

CLICK

UH OH...

THE SKY IS A DEEP ORANGE! CALVIN'S SKIN IS A PALE GREEN! YELLOW FLOWERS ARE NOW BLUE!

EVERY COLOR IS THE OPPOSITE OF WHAT IT SHOULD BE!

CALVIN HAS BEEN TRANSFERRED TO A COLOR FILM NEGATIVE!

HIS ONLY HOPE IS TO BE PROCESSED BY A 1-HOUR PHOTO FINISHER! DEVELOPER! I NEED DEVELOPER!

DOGGONE IT, CALVIN! THAT'S *ANOTHER* PICTURE RUINED! CAN'T YOU LOOK PLEASANT FOR 1/500TH OF A SECOND?!

Calvin and Hobbes
by WATTERSON

AHH... A DAY AT THE LAKE! THIS WILL BE GREAT!

I STILL DON'T SEE WHY WE CAN'T JUST SIT IN THE CAR WITH THE AIR CONDITIONER ON.

I'M GETTING SAND IN MY SUIT! I DON'T WANT TO SIT ON THE BEACH!

THIS WATER'S TOO COLD! I'M FREEZING TO DEATH!

OUT HERE THERE'S TOO MUCH SUN! I'LL GET SUNBURNED!

THIS LOTION MAKES ME GREASY AND MY SHIRT MAKES ME TOO HOT!

I DON'T WANT TO SIT IN THE SHADE! THIS IS BORING!

I HATE WALKING! MY LEGS ARE TIRED AND THE SAND IS TOO HOT AND THE WATER IS TOO COLD AND THERE'S NO SHADE HERE AND I'VE STILL GOT SAND IN MY SUIT!

WHAT? ARE WE GOING ALREADY?

WATTERSON

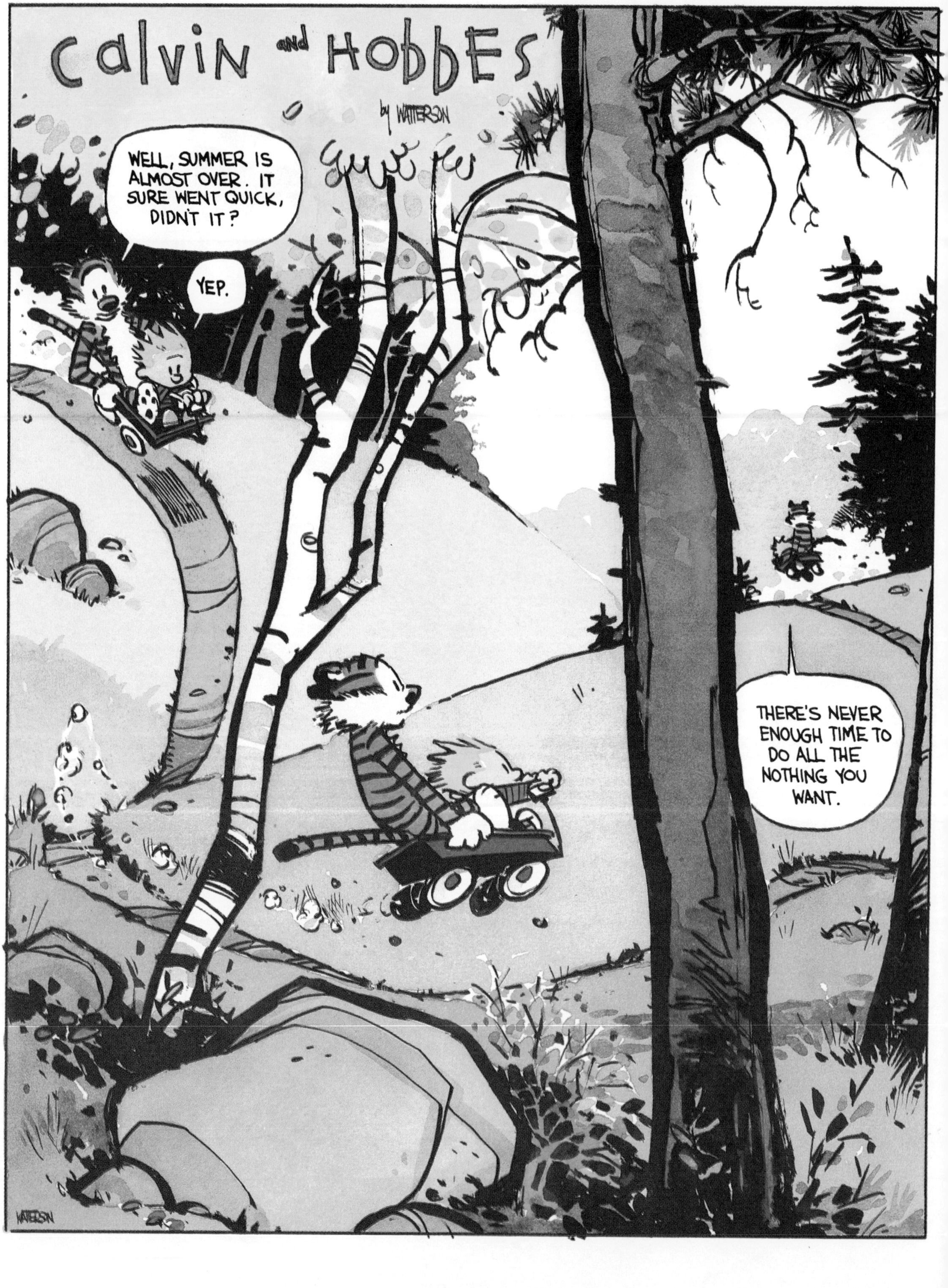
Calvin and HOBBES
by WATTERSON
WELL, SUMMER IS ALMOST OVER. IT SURE WENT QUICK, DIDN'T IT?
YEP.
THERE'S NEVER ENOUGH TIME TO DO ALL THE NOTHING YOU WANT.
WATTERSON

# AFTERWORD

Long ago the Sunday comics were printed the size of an entire newspaper page. Each comic was like a color poster. Not surprisingly, with all that space to fill, cartoonists produced works of incredible beauty and power that we just don't see anymore, now that strips are a third or a quarter of their former size. Whereas Little Nemo could dream through 15 surreal panels back in the early part of the century, today it's rare to see a Sunday strip with more than six panels—especially if the characters move. All the things that make comics fun to read—the stories, the dialogue, the pictures—have gotten simpler and simpler in order to keep the work legible at smaller and smaller sizes. The art form has been in a process of retrograde evolution for decades. For those of us trying to return some of the childhood fun we had marveling at comic drawings, the opportunities today are discouraging.

Cartoons can be much more than we've been seeing lately. How much more will depend on what newspaper readers will demand. One thing, though, is certain: little boys, like tigers, will roam all the territory they can get.

—BILL WATTERSON

# The End